Baptized In The Spirit

FRANK M. BOYD

Radiant Life

1445 Boonville Avenue
Springfield, MO 65802-1894
02-0111

STAFF

Editor in Chief: Gary Leggett
Series Editor: Clancy Hayes
Assistant Editors: Lori Horne
Gerald Parks
Editorial Assistants: Diane Lamb
Terry Bryant
Design : Steve Lopez
Marilyn Jansen
Don Burchfield

Photo Credits:
PhotoDisc, Inc.: Cover, pp. 1, 2, 3, 4, 5, 6, 7, 56, 81, Back Cover;
Rubber Ball: p. 17, Digital Stock, Inc: Cover, p. 9, Back Cover;
Ricky Davis: pp. 26, 34, 42, 65, 75; Israel Bureau of Tourism: p. 48.

Second Printing 2004
©1996 by the Gospel Publishing House
Springfield, Missouri 65802-1894
Adapted from *The Holy Spirit* by Frank M. Boyd

Library Of Congress Catalog Card Number 95-79379
ISBN 0-88243-111-0
Printed in the United States of America

A Leader's Guide for individual or group study with this book is available
(order number 02-0211). ISBN: 0-88243-211-7

CONTENTS

WELCOME TO THE

SPIRITUAL *Discovery* SERIES

We are glad you have chosen to study with us. We believe the discoveries you make through the use of the *Spiritual Discovery Series* will positively impact your life.

The *Spiritual Discovery Series* will challenge the user to ask questions of the biblical text, discover principles from the text, and make personal application of those truths. The Bible is the text. This guide is a tool for study.

The *Spiritual Discovery Series* is designed for use in either individual or group settings. Individuals will be excited by the discoveries made possible through a structured inductive study. Sunday School classes and other groups will find the *Spiritual Discovery Series* a valuable tool for promoting enlightened discussions centered on biblical truth.

HOW TO USE THIS STUDY GUIDE

1 Pray before beginning each study session. Ask the Holy Spirit to illuminate your mind.

2 Choose a translation of the Bible which you trust and can understand. It will be helpful to have more than one translation available to aid your understanding of the biblical text.

3 The Bible is your primary text. Avoid using commentaries or reference books until after completing your own study. Reference works are best used to confirm your findings. On occasion, the study guide will direct you to use reference material. This is done when special insights are necessary for proper interpretation.

4 Read the assigned biblical text at least twice before answering any questions. This will provide an overview and focus on God's Word.

5 Concentrate on the biblical passage which you are studying. It is tempting to jump from one passage of Scripture to another in an attempt to make spiritual connections.

6 Seek tangible ways to apply the principles gleaned from each study. Bible study should never result in "head knowledge" alone. Bible study should lead to action.

WHO IS THE HOLY SPIRIT?

We are living in an age when the Holy Spirit is the active Agent of the Triune God. We ought to know Him in His real nature, in His attributes, in His names, and in His ministries. All matters and questions pertaining to the doctrine of the Holy Spirit, therefore, should be of unusual interest to us who live in this period of special spiritual privilege.

It is vitally important that we know the Holy Spirit not as an impersonal force, but as a divine Person—the third Person of the Trinity. He possesses the attributes of deity, so is properly designated God, the Spirit. He is presented in Scripture under various names and symbols.

THE NATURE OF THE HOLY SPIRIT

What constitutes personality? It is difficult to define personality when used of the divine Being, since God cannot be measured. But there are certain elements in personality that we can identify—intellect, sensibility, and will.

Intellect involves the mind and is the power of reasoning, judging, comprehending, etc. It is distinguished from sensibility, which is the power to feel or receive sensation, impressions, pleasurable or painful; and from will, which is the power of choosing or acting, the power of self-determination.

Obviously, when one possesses the attributes, properties, and qualities of personality, then that being can be said to have personality. Does the Holy Spirit possess such properties? We shall see.

✎ 1. Read John 14:16,17,26. How does Jesus refer to the Holy Spirit in these verses and what does this indicate about His view of the personhood of the Holy Spirit?

_____

_____

Jesus promised the disciples He would ask God, the Father, to send another to do for the disciples what He had done for them. The term *Comforter* cannot be used of any abstract, impersonal influence or force. This is clear from 1 John 2:1, where the same word—translated "advocate"—is used of Christ. No one but a person can take the place of a person. No mere impersonal influence could take the place of Jesus Christ, the greatest personality that ever lived.

The Holy Spirit is referred to with the masculine pronoun *ekeinos* 12 times in John 16. The same word is used of Christ in 1 John 2:6; 3:3,5,7,16. Here is a clear-cut statement affirming the personality of the Holy Spirit.

A further proof of the personality of the Holy Spirit can be found in His identification with the Father, the Son, and with Christians. In the baptismal pronouncement (Matthew 28:19) and in the apostolic benediction (2 Corinthians 13:14) the Holy Spirit is identified with the Father and the Son in such a way as to imply personality—not mere abstract power or force.

✎ 2. Read Acts 15:22-29. What does the stated relationship between the Church leaders and the Holy Spirit indicate about their perception of the personhood of the Holy Spirit?

_____

_____

The Holy Spirit is described in Scripture in such a way as to leave no doubt as to His personality. He exercises the attributes of personality: mind (Romans 8:27), will (1 Corinthians 12:11), and feeling (Ephesians 4:30). Personal activities are ascribed to Him: He reveals (2 Peter 1:21), teaches (John 14:26), witnesses (Galatians 4:6), intercedes (Romans 8:26), speaks (Revelation 2:7), commands

(Acts 16:6,7), and testifies (John 15:26). He is susceptible to personal treatment: He may be grieved (Ephesians 4:30), lied to (Acts 5:3), and blasphemed (Matthew 12:31,32). Again, some impersonal force or power could not interact in these ways.

3. Why is it important for us to know and understand who the Holy Spirit is? (1 Corinthians 2:9-14).

_____

_____

_____

As important as the establishment of the personal nature of the Holy Spirit is, we must not forget that He is divine as well.

4. Read the following passages and record the titles used when referring to the Holy Spirit.

Acts 5:3,4 _____

_____

2 Corinthians 3:18 _____

_____

How do these titles affirm the deity of the Holy Spirit? _____

_____

The Holy Spirit is described in various ways which indicate His divine nature.

5. List the characteristics ascribed to the Holy Spirit in the following verses.

Psalm 139:7-10 _____

_____

Luke 1:35 _____

_____

1 Corinthians 2:10,11 _____

_____

Hebrews 9:14 _____

_____

✎ 6. The Holy Spirit also performs divine works. Read the following passages and list the miraculous activity recorded there.

Genesis 1:2 _____

_____

Job 33:4 _____

_____

Psalm 104:30 _____

_____

John 3:5-8 _____

_____

_____

THE NAMES OF THE HOLY SPIRIT

The Bible refers to the Holy Spirit by a variety of names. Each reveals aspects of who He is and the function He plays in the Trinity. It is instructive to review the various names in order to become better acquainted with Him.

✎ 7. How do the following Scripture passages refer to the Holy Spirit?

Acts 1:4 _The promise of the Father_

Acts 1:6,7 _____

Romans 8:2 _Spirit of life_

Romans 14:17 _RIGHTEOUSNESS, PEACE AND JOY_

Galatians 4:5,6 _SPIRIT OF THE SON (ADOPTION)_

Ephesians 4:30 _____

Hebrews 10:29 _____

1 John 4:2 _____

Let's examine some of the names of the Holy Spirit used in Scripture. One of the more common names is "the Spirit of God" and is used to indicate the fact He has a definite relation to God the Father. As the representative or agent of God the Father, the Holy Spirit does the work of the Father here on earth.

✎ 8. From the following Scriptures, determine the functions the Holy Spirit executes on behalf of God the Father.

John 6:44 _____

_____

_____

John 16:13 _____

_____

_____

Romans 8:14 _____

_____

_____

Another way Scripture refers to the Holy Spirit is as "the Spirit of Christ." Some have wondered if the variations of this name, "Spirit of Christ," "Spirit of Jesus Christ," and "Spirit of Jesus," indicate a multiplicity of Spirits distinct from one another.

✎ 9. Compare and contrast Romans 8:9; 1 Corinthians 3:16; and 1 Corinthians 12:3. Note below how they address the question of multiple spirits.

_____

_____

_____

_____

The Holy Spirit is called "the Spirit of Christ" because He is sent in the name of Christ (John 14:26), because He is the Spirit sent by Christ (John 15:26), and because His special mission in this age is to glorify Christ (John 16:14).

The Holy Spirit is also called "the Comforter." This name is given to the Holy Spirit who came to assist the disciples after Jesus' ascension. The Holy Spirit is a personal friend, a wonderful teacher, a companion, and guide—One who would be there to meet their spiritual needs.

The most common name used of the third member of the Trinity is simply "the Holy Spirit." The emphasis here is on holiness. He, equally with the Father and the Son, shares divine attributes. The most glorious attribute or quality of God is His holiness. The designation *Holy* affirms that in Him resides the all-pervading Spirit, the blazing fire of the purity and holiness of Almighty God. By His power the believer is enabled to live a life of victory over sin. Holiness is an outstanding characteristic of the Holy Spirit.

Three times the Holy Spirit is designated by Jesus as "the Spirit of Truth" (John 14:17; 15:26; 16:13). Just as God is love—the very embodiment of infinite love in an infinite Being, so the Spirit is truth—the personification of truth, as opposed to "the spirit of error" in the world, inspired by Satan (1 John 4:6).

Since Christ himself is truth (John 14:6) and the Spirit is truth, He is the One who glorifies and interprets Christ.

The Holy Spirit is referred to as "the Spirit of grace" in Hebrews 10:29. The whole gospel is a gospel of grace, and as the executive of the Godhead, the Spirit grants grace. All God's gifts are divine endowments finding their source in His grace (Greek—*charis*). No merit of any kind or degree can be presented to Him in payment for His gifts. He dispenses the grace or unmerited favor of God.

The Holy Spirit operates in the lives of believers as "the Spirit of life." As the Spirit of life He makes us free from "the law of sin and death." The Holy Spirit is the flow of divine life which pours into our lives overcoming the law of sin and death. This virtue is from heaven representing a more abundant life, and it comes in the Person of the Holy Spirit. He refreshes our physical bodies (Romans 8:11) and through Him comes divine healing (1 Corinthians 12:9).

The special work of establishing sinners in the family of God as His legal heirs is a particular ministry of the Holy Spirit. The word *adoption* in the original Greek is an interesting word, meaning literally "the placing of sons." It comes from two words *huios* (hwe-os)—son, and *thesis*—a placing. Our birth into the family of God is expressed by another Greek word *teknon,* which John uses frequently to express a relation based upon community of nature. He never uses the word *huios* to describe the relation of Christians to God, since their position is not a result of adoption, but a new life.

Paul, on the other hand regards their relationship as a legal adoption imparting a new dignity and position. The whole thought of adoption is standing in a completeness of relation to God as sons.

✎ 10. Read the following biblical passages on adoption, then record your findings on how the Spirit is involved in establishing our adoption into the family of God: Romans 8:15-17,23; Galatians 4:1-7; Ephesians 1:5,13,14.

_____

_____

_____

✎ 11. The names given to the Holy Spirit in Scripture are very descriptive in explaining who He is. Looking only at the titles ascribed to Him, what can we say about His ministry?

_____

_____

_____

_____

THE SYMBOLS OF THE HOLY SPIRIT

In the same way the names of the Holy Spirit are instructive concerning the identity of the Holy Spirit, an examination of the various symbols used to describe Him will provide important insights.

✎ **12. What symbols of the Holy Spirit are used in Acts 2:1-4?**

_____

_____

An important symbol often associated with the Holy Spirit is fire. Fire is a great consumer as well as a great refiner. All that is worthless and impure is burned out by the Holy Spirit's cleansing presence and the soul is set afire with a burning passion and zeal to serve God. That passion, zeal, and power were represented on the Day of Pentecost by the "tongues of fire" which appeared on the heads of the 120 baptized in the Spirit on that day. That which cannot be refined and purged by divine holiness will ultimately be destroyed from the presence of that holiness.

Wind is significant as the symbol of the Holy Spirit because wind is invisible to the eye, yet visible in the effects of His power. The Greek word *pneuma*, referring to the Holy Spirit, is translated "spirit," the ordinary Greek word for wind, air, or breath.

✎ **13. What was the result of "divine" breath in Genesis 2:7 and John 20:22?**

_____

_____

_____

The Holy Spirit is present everywhere just as is the air we breathe. He is our life. He is the life-imparting Spirit. As the breath or wind of God, He filled the waiting disciples on the Day of Pentecost. The wind that blew through the Upper Room gave life to an organism which would become the Church.

✎ **14. What is the work of the Holy Spirit compared to in the following verses?**

Ephesians 1:13 _____

_____

_____

2 Timothy 2:19 _____

_____

The symbol of a seal conveys many thoughts which demonstrate the work of the Holy Spirit. Following are just a few:

Ownership. The imprint of a seal implies a relation to the owner of the seal, and is a token of something belonging to him. Believers are identified with God and known to be so by His Spirit dwelling in them.

The following custom was common in Ephesus in Paul's day. A merchant would go to the harbor, select certain timber and then stamp it with his seal—an acknowledged sign of ownership. Later he would send his servant with his signet to locate the timber bearing the corresponding impression. So our possession and ownership by God are declared by the seal of the Holy Spirit.

Genuineness and authority. Official documents are validated by the seal of the nation or jurisdiction. When Jesus was buried, the chief priests made the sepulcher sure by sealing the stone and setting a watch (Matthew 27:66). To tamper with that seal was an implied attack on the Roman government. If anyone attacks the *sealed* child of God, he attacks the heavenly authority which endorses him as genuine.

Security or preservation. Canned fruits and vegetables are sealed from outside air, so they remain preserved as long as the seal is unbroken. This is comparable to our lives being sealed by His Spirit to keep out the evil influences of this world.

Oil is another symbol of the Holy Spirit. Whenever oil was used to anoint in the Old Testament, it spoke of usefulness, fruitfulness, beauty, life, and transformation.

15. **How does the previous information concerning oil help your understanding of Luke 4:18; Acts 10:38; and 1 John 2:20,27?**

_____

_____

16. **How is the Holy Spirit pictured in Matthew 3:16,17?**

_____

_____

_____

This symbol speaks of gentleness, tenderness, loveliness, innocence, mildness, peace, purity, and patience.

SUMMARY

The blessed Holy Spirit—the Third Person of the Trinity—is the great Executive and Administrator of the Godhead in the Church today. How important it is to know Him as a divine Person, who has the right to exercise sovereignty over each believer. We have seen how the Holy Spirit is the active representative from the throne of God today. Without His work and ministry in our lives, we would not know or experience the relationship with God that is ours to enjoy.

Throughout the Bible we see the impact of the Holy Spirit. His influence is seen in providing God's people with help, direction, comfort, power, and instruction. His ministry has not stopped. He desires to be as active in our lives today as we are willing to let Him have a part.

LET'S REVIEW

✎ 1. Why is it important to know the true nature of the Holy Spirit?

_____

_____

_____

✎ 2. What Scriptures verify the personality of the Holy Spirit?

_____

_____

_____

✎ 3. Where can you find evidence of the deity of the Holy Spirit?

_____

_____

_____

✎ 4. Give the names and symbols of the Holy Spirit which represent His most recent work in your life. Give a brief account of that activity.

_____

_____

_____

✎ 5. When did you first realize the nature and character of the Holy Spirit, and how did that impact your life?

_____

_____

_____

_____

STUDY 2

THE MINISTRY OF THE HOLY SPIRIT

Each member of the Godhead or Trinity has a specific responsibility as the Father, Son, and Holy Spirit work together to complete the will of God. The role of the Holy Spirit is to facilitate God's will on earth by interacting with followers of Christ.

The Holy Spirit, with His ministries, is God's gift to fallen man. The Spirit first convicts of sin; then He regenerates, sanctifies, baptizes, and ministers in the everyday aspects of life.

In this study, we will examine the specific functions which have been assigned to the Holy Spirit which assist Christians to live victorious lives.

THE HOLY SPIRIT LEADS US TO THE SAVIOR

God loves His creation. When man yielded to the temptation of sin (Genesis 3), God quickly set in place a plan of recovery for humanity. He arranged for the necessary sacrifice for the payment of sin—His Son Jesus Christ. He also provided the Holy Spirit who would direct unredeemed man to the Son. Man's role in the process is to recognize his need of a Savior.

✎ 1. Read John 16:8. How does the Holy Spirit help individuals see their need of a Savior?

_____

_____

The first step in the divine process of bringing an individual into a personal relationship with God is conviction. Man's sin alienates him from God, blinds his spiritual eyes, and leaves him helpless and hopeless. The initiative in man's recovery must be from God, for man in his sinful state has no inclination to seek God.

✎ 2. Read John 16:9. According to this verse, what is the basis of all sin?

_____

_____

Throughout the years, man has tried to come up with other grounds for his sinful behavior. Some point to dysfunctional homes, disadvantaged circumstances, or a lack of education. These excuses seek to nullify the need for conviction of sin and repentance by man. The net result of this type of thinking is despair and hopelessness.

✎ 3. How can identifying the true source of sin provide hope for the hopeless?

_____

_____

The world's conduct toward Jesus, when He came to earth, is the decisive proof of its sinfulness. The Cross reveals what human nature is capable of—subjecting the embodiment of love to the shame, rejection, and suffering of Calvary. The Holy Spirit has come to bring that reality to the world's collective consciousness.

✎ 4. Again, read John 16:9. Jesus came to earth as a contrast to the unrighteousness of the world. What is the proof given for the righteousness of Jesus?

_____

_____

The resurrection and ascension of Jesus was a vindication of himself and His mission. Those who align themselves with Jesus and His teachings can be assured that they are participating in righteousness.

To be convicted of righteousness is of little importance unless we are convinced that righteousness will finally be victorious.

Satan has been contending against God from the beginning of the world. Satan wants to possess all that God has created. A primary target of Satan's attack was humanity because God had given the first humans authority to rule the earth. Satan succeeded temporarily in dethroning humanity and became the *prince of this world.* This world is his usurped principality.

✎ 5. Read John 16:9 again. According to this verse, what is the present condition of Satan?

_____

_____

The second Adam—the man Christ Jesus—overthrew the prince of this world by His incarnation and His death. Satan has already been judged, and he will be banished into the lake of fire forever. The Holy Spirit convinces us of this triumph by Christ. We are free from the accusations, the bondage, and the tyranny of Satan. Let's rejoice in it, act upon it, and assert our freedom in Christ!

When a person answers the Holy Spirit's tug on his heart, God performs three simultaneous works. He recreates a new nature which is dead to sin and alive to righteousness, He justifies those who were previously condemned, and He adopts individuals who were once children of the devil into God's family. The classic passage on regeneration is found in the third chapter of John, the account of Jesus and Nicodemus.

✎ 6. According to John 3:2, what conclusion did Nicodemus make about Jesus and on what basis did he make it?

_____

_____

_____

Nicodemus was a Pharisee, a ruler of the Jews and a member of the Sanhedrin—the governing council of the Jews. He witnessed the miracles Jesus performed in Jerusalem at the Passover feast and was convinced Jesus was no ordinary man. He wanted to be a part of the kingdom of God of which Jesus spoke. He doubtless thought himself eligible for the kingdom of God because of his legacy from Abraham.

✎ 7. How did Jesus respond to Nicodemus' request? (John 3:3).

_____

_____

8. What is the role of the Holy Spirit in the rebirth process according to John 3:5-8 and Titus 3:4,5?

_____

_____

Nicodemus was a good man—moral and religious—yet Jesus insisted he begin life again, or be born a second time. Man's nature, warped by sin, must undergo a change so radical it is actually a second birth. Nicodemus doubted the possibility of a second birth.

9. How did Jesus respond when Nicodemus expressed surprise? (John 3:10-21). Read Ezekiel 36:25-27 to see what Jesus assumed Nicodemus already understood.

_____

_____

Being born of the Spirit is a profound mystery. Just as Jesus pointed out the mystery of the moving of the wind, so it is with the moving of the Holy Spirit upon human nature. Just as God breathed the breath of life into man's inanimate form, so man's spirit _dead in trespasses and sins_, is touched by the Spirit of God and made to come alive. It is only then that man can begin to respond to a spiritual world previously unknown and grow in Christ.

Sanctification means setting apart something for exclusive use. The priests of the Levitical order of worship were set apart to the sacred ministry of the tabernacle and the temple. Appointed and chosen by God, they ministered both to God and the people in the sacrificial order of worship. Certain vessels were sanctified for use exclusively in worship. All the furniture and vessels were set apart for sacred use. When a person accepts Jesus as Savior, he commits himself to a life of sanctification. To split his commitment between Jesus and the world is an act of spiritual adultery.

10. Read 2 Thessalonians 2:13. Who is the source of our sanctification?

_____

11. Read 1 Peter 1:2. What is the purpose of sanctification?

_____

_____

Sanctification does not occur instantaneously. It is a process of being transformed into the likeness of Christ, dying to our sinful nature, and becoming alive to righteousness. The Holy Spirit works in the saved person to direct him away from sin and toward God. He warns with conviction when temptation is faced, then encourages obedience and submission to God. He guides in truth and righteousness and brings maturity and spiritual fruitfulness to the Christian.

The Holy Spirit is called holy because He is absolutely holy himself, and because He makes believers holy. It is the Spirit's work to war against the desires of the flesh and to produce fruit leading to holiness.

✎ 12. Read Galatians 5:17-22. What does this passage teach concerning sanctification and holiness?

_____

_____

✎ 13. Read Romans 7:1 to 8:39. How many times is the Holy Spirit mentioned in each chapter?

_____

✎ 14. How is the Holy Spirit portrayed in each of these chapters?

_____

THE HOLY SPIRIT HELPS US MATURE SPIRITUALLY

The Book of Genesis records that the Lord often revealed His presence to Adam and Eve before the Fall. Many Scriptures reveal His desire for fellowship with mankind. His infinite heart is satisfied only as He is permitted to indwell the life of His creation (Isaiah 57:15,16; 66:1,2).

In the Old Testament, the presence of God was exhibited objectively (external), rather than subjectively (internal). He manifested himself to Israel in the pillar of cloud and fire which covered the camp and later filled the tabernacle and the Temple of Solomon.

✎ 15. According to Romans 8:9; 1 Corinthians 3:16; 6:19, what tabernacle or temple does the Holy Spirit reside in now?

_____

_____

Although the presence of God appeared to man and Christ physically walked among His followers, the Holy Spirit has been the secret Presence of God within the creation. He has been the Source of life amid the chaos, bringing form and order from what was shapeless and void. He has been the Voice of truth in the hearts of all rational beings and resides in His temple; the heart of the Christian.

Jesus was careful to explain to His disciples the process that would be used to continue their spiritual growth and development after He left the earth. The Holy Spirit was to be their primary ally. Let's look at the role of the Holy Spirit both then and now.

16. According to John 14:26, what was a primary ministry of the Holy Spirit to the disciples, as well as to us today?

_____

_____

A key to spiritual growth is knowledge. The Holy Spirit is commissioned to be our spiritual teacher. He does not come to reveal new truth to us, for all truth has already been revealed in Christ. History tells us that external revelation of truth is usually not enough for us. What we know is usually greater than our internal compliance or our external obedience to that knowledge. Natural man has a difficult time understanding spiritual truth.

As a Teacher, the work of the Holy Spirit is a continuation of the prophetic office of Christ. Jesus is the Great Teacher, but the Holy Spirit is His representative on earth during Jesus' personal absence from His people on earth.

Just as the Spirit recalled to mind and illuminated truth given by Christ to the disciples, He illuminates the truth of the Word to our hearts. He teaches us by the Word which He inspired the apostles to write.

17. Read 1 Corinthians 2:6-15; 2 Timothy 3:16,17; and 2 Peter 1:20,21. What two important functions has the Holy Spirit been involved in with the Word of God?

_____

_____

He gives us His teaching in response to our prayer for a fervent longing for truth, benefiting both our natural and our spiritual lives. He is an infallible Teacher; there is no one like Him. He is an ever-present Teacher. Let us keep our hearts responsive to His faithful, precious instructions.

18. Record below the promise found in Romans 8:14.

_____

_____

History reveals how far astray man can go when he is not guided by divine power. Failed leadership and oppression, war and revolution, economic disruption, class strife, and individual disharmony all result from man's effort to guide and govern himself.

In this modern day of sophisticated weaponry, man possesses vast and uncontrollable powers of self-destruction. Man left to himself is like a person in a vast jungle or in a howling wilderness without a guide.

The Spirit of God is fully qualified to guide the Christian. He knows life's journey with all its intricacies and dangers. He has provided a road map through the written Word of God (2 Peter 1:21).

19. Read 1 Corinthians 2:10. What is required of those who wish to know God?

_____

_____

For the Spirit to lead an individual, a spiritual life must be present. The Holy Spirit does not lead someone who is alive to sin and dead to Christ. There must be a total dependence upon the Holy Spirit for His leading, as opposed to trusting in our own abilities and knowledge to take us where we want to go. The Spirit leads us from ourselves and our own righteousness to Christ, the answer to each and every one of our needs.

The Spirit leads us to truth. There are many voices in the world today that claim to be the answer for this life. The Spirit of Truth can take us through differing opinions, conflicting creeds, and replace confusion with understanding based upon the revealed Word of God.

The Spirit directs us to a life of holiness. His goal is to help us become more Christlike in all aspects of our life.

The Spirit also leads to comfort, no matter the circumstances. Whatever life may have to offer, He will take us to the grace, peace, and love that is found in Christ. There are many other powerful influences trying to compete with the Holy Spirit. We must not give our honor, love, and devotion to any other than the One who will lead us to Christ.

20. Read the following Scriptures and list some of the benefits which come from our association with the Holy Spirit (John 14:16,17,26,27; John 15:26; 2 Corinthians 1:3,4; and 1 Thessalonians 1:6).

_____

_____

The title _Comforter_, referring to the Holy Spirit, means more than just One who gives sympathy and soothes us in time of sorrow or discouragement. As our Comforter, He is to be to us all that Jesus was to His disciples. There was no phase of their lives into which Jesus did not enter, and there is no phase of our lives with which the Holy Spirit is unacquainted and where He does not faithfully minister.

The disciples told Jesus their troubles and perplexities; we must trust the Comforter with ours. Whenever they felt baffled by Satan, they relied upon their Leader's power; so we must call on the aid of the Holy Spirit. When they needed guidance, they sought direction from Jesus; we must also seek and abide by the Spirit's leadings. When they knew what to do, but were too weak to carry it out, they waited upon the Master for strength; so must we wait upon the Spirit of all grace for His enabling.

The Spirit comforts by His indwelling presence. It is through His ministry we enjoy the peace of God. That quiet, dignified poise keeps us calm in the midst of exasperating circumstances of an attack of the enemy of our souls.

Although known as the Comforter, the Holy Spirit never gives an individual rest in his sin. He is always active to convict a person of it and to separate him from it. He is not like an indulgent parent who avoids rebellion and unpleasantness and fails to reprove his child. The Holy Spirit endeavors to remove the cause of the evil.

Spurgeon, one of Christendom's great preachers, has said, "Do not expect to get comfort by merely running to sweet texts or listening to pleasing preachers; but expect to find comfort through the holy, reproving, humbling, strengthening, sanctifying processes which are the operation of the Divine Paraclete. His comfort is not founded upon concealment. Some have obtained consolation by conveniently forgetting troublesome truth. Now, the Holy Spirit lays the whole truth open before us; therefore our consolation is not of fools, but of wise men; peace, which age and experience will not invalidate, but which both these will deepen, causing it to grow with our growth and strengthen with our strength."

✎ 21. What does the Bible teach regarding God's approach to sickness? (Exodus 15:26; Psalm 103:1-5; Matthew 4:23,24; 8:16,17; James 5:14-16).

_____

_____

There is a wide difference between a sickness and a sin. Sin is the deliberate choice of wrong. Sicknesses are those inherent physical, mental, or emotional disabilities and inclinations, which sin has created, but for which individuals may not be directly responsible.

The Word of God clearly reveals God's sympathies with man's diseases. Although this is the case, we cannot excuse ourselves or others for wrongdoing which leads to diseases. The knowledge of the Holy Spirit's sympathy for us should hasten us to seek a higher, holier, and nobler life. There may be much against us—the conditions of birth, early education, and habit trends formed early—but God is for us. He, by His Spirit, knows us and helps our infirmities.

✎ 22. Christians often feel weak in their ability to effectively communicate with God. What remedy is provided in Romans 8:26,27?

_____

_____

What hope the Holy Spirit provides in times of weakness! We cannot fully understand how this works, or the power that is at work on our behalf. But we can be sure that He will be there when we need His strength.

SUMMARY

What would we do without the ministry of the Holy Spirit? We would have been forever alienated from God had the Holy Spirit not come to show us our lost condition.

Be thankful for His ministries in your life as He shapes you into the image and likeness of Jesus and yield to His desires so this work will not be hindered. Embrace the Holy Spirit for the needs of your mortal bodies, and look joyously and confidently for that day when He will energize the whole body of Christ to be translated into the presence of God.

LET'S REVIEW

✎ 1. List the three steps which the Holy Spirit takes in bringing a soul to God.

_____

_____

_____

_____

✎ 2. Describe the operation of the Holy Spirit in the process of sanctification.

_____

_____

_____

_____

✎ 3. Discuss ways the Holy Spirit leads Christians into a deeper relationship with Jesus.

_____

_____

_____

_____

_____

✎ 4. How have you been led by the ministry of the Spirit?

_____

_____

_____

_____

_____

_____

STUDY 3

COME HOLY SPIRIT

We will look at various aspects of the baptism in the Holy Spirit in the next several studies. This study will focus on the promise of an outpouring of the Spirit, the fulfillment of that promise, and its application in the lives of those who willingly receive it.

The main purpose of the coming of the Holy Spirit to the Church in fullness on the Day of Pentecost was to empower believers to communicate the gospel message. The baptism in the Spirit is available to God's people today to accomplish the very same purpose.

THE PROMISED OUTPOURING

The classic Old Testament passage concerning the promise of an outpouring of the Holy Spirit is Joel 2:28-32. We do not know exactly when Joel prophesied, but it was to the southern kingdom of Judah, around 770 B.C. Joel was probably the first of the great prophets to speak of Jehovah's message to Judah.

1. Read Joel 2:21-28. When will the Spirit be poured out according to this passage?

_____

_____

_____

Joel prophesied during a time when natural calamities had fallen upon Western Asia and Joel identifies them. He refers to the plague of locusts that devastated the land, followed by drought and famine, and he applies this to a spiritual truth.

2. Considering the context of Joel's message, who do you think Joel was promising would receive the outpouring of the Spirit?

_____

_____

_____

_____

_____

Part of this passage is often quoted in connection with the wonders of the Day of Pentecost. It has become so familiar to us that we have almost lost the meaning intended in its original context.

3. Why are people tempted to bypass the importance of Joel's message to his original audience in favor of those present at the Day of Pentecost? (Acts 2:14-21).

_____

_____

_____

_____

_____

✎ 4. Reread Joel 2:1-27. What were the conditions for having the Holy Spirit poured out on all people?

_____

_____

_____

✎ 5. What spiritual results are promised once the Spirit is poured out?

_____

_____

_____

The language used by Joel brings images of liquid drenching those who encounter the Spirit. This imagery was employed by John the Baptist when he spoke of a baptism with the Spirit.

✎ 6. What promise of John the Baptist is recorded in Matthew 3:11,12?

_____

_____

_____

The word *baptize* is a Greek word that means "to immerse." In classical Greek literature, the word *baptize* is used to describe the sinking of ships, of crowds overwhelming a city, and metaphorically of being drowned in drink. The expression *baptized with* or *in the Holy Spirit* means "to be immersed, sunk, overwhelmed in the medium or person of the Holy Spirit."

John's baptism was introductory and transitory; Christ's baptism was to be spiritual, quickening, and searching. John's baptism was an outward washing with no inward grace. It was only a symbol. Christ's baptism would be an immersion with an inward reality, a living, glorious, inward grace.

✎ 7. In Acts 1:4,5,8, what were the last things Jesus mentioned to His followers before His ascension?

_____

_____

_____

8. Compare and contrast Jesus' words recorded in Acts 1:4,5,8 with the words of John the Baptist recorded in Matthew 3:11,12. Record your discoveries below.

_____

_____

_____

_____

_____

An outpouring of the Holy Spirit was promised during the Old Testament era and during the time of Jesus. The prerequisite for this outpouring was the same in both situations. It is important for those living in the present age to know that God continues to promise an outpouring of the Holy Spirit for those who will repent of their sins and draw close to Him.

THE PROMISE FULFILLED

9. Read Acts 2:2-4. What three significant signs were present at the initial visitation of the baptism in the Spirit?

_____

_____

_____

In both the Hebrew and the Greek the words for wind and for Spirit are the same. The Holy Spirit is the mighty breath of God, which pervades all the universe and brings life to all creation, inanimate, and animate—vegetation, animal life, humankind.

10. Why is the wind a good symbol to describe the person of the Holy Spirit? (John 3:8).

_____

_____

_____

_____

The wind of the Spirit on the Day of Pentecost was a *rushing* one, portraying the Spirit's rapid influence, rushing like a torrent. Within 50 years of the Day of

Pentecost the gospel had been preached in every country of the known world. It was mighty and irresistible, just as the Spirit of God is. Where He comes nothing can stand against Him.

"Tongues of fire" (NIV) appeared over each person who was filled with the Spirit. The phenomenon was reminiscent of the pillar of fire which rested over the camp of Israel of old. Suddenly this phenomenon divided, and separate tongues of fire rested upon the head of each of the 120 present. This wonder of fire, frequently mentioned in the Old Testament accompanying Deity, assured the disciples that this power was divine.

Those who received the baptism in the Holy Spirit spoke with other tongues or languages other than what they knew. This was an appropriate initial physical evidence because the purpose of the baptism in the Holy Spirit was to make believers witnesses (Acts 1:8).

11. Read Acts 2:5-12. In what practical way did speech in unknown languages serve to fulfill the purpose of the baptism in the Holy Spirit on the Day of Pentecost?

_____

_____

This phenomenon of speaking with tongues was startling to those present on that special day at the end of the Feast of Weeks.

12. What was the explanation the unsaved gave for the events that occurred on the Day of Pentecost? (Acts 2:13).

_____

_____

Among the crowd gathered on that day were some who mocked, not even inquiring as to the meaning of the phenomenon of that occasion. A miracle of the Holy Spirit was made an object of derision. This was dangerous ground to be on.

13. In the Acts 2:14-36 account, what did Peter say had just happened to the believers?

_____

_____

14. Compare the person described in Matthew 26:69-75 with the man who preached on the Day of Pentecost (Acts 2:14-36). How is he different? How might this difference be explained?

_____

_____

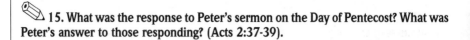 **15. What was the response to Peter's sermon on the Day of Pentecost? What was Peter's answer to those responding? (Acts 2:37-39).**

_____

_____

There can be no honest mistaking the meaning of Peter's words. Here God was about to confirm a threefold covenant in sending the Holy Spirit: (1) a national covenant to the Jewish listeners on Pentecost and to the nation—God's covenant people whom they represented; (2) a family covenant—to your children, those then living and the generations to follow; (3) a universal covenant—to all that are far off, even as many as the Lord our God shall call, to the Gentiles and to every individual who would respond to the call of God through the gospel.

The expression "to all that are far off" was used by the rabbis to refer to the Gentiles. With Pentecost as a beginning, God was about to bring every nation into the covenant of redemption.

The glorious experience of the baptism in the Holy Spirit was appointed by God for every believer from the Day of Pentecost to the Church today. The infilling of the Spirit, testified to by the speaking with tongues, is the pattern for that experience for every believer throughout His Church. This was God's promise for your opportunity to receive the baptism in the Holy Spirit today.

THE PROMISE APPLIED

The symbolism of pouring water and terms related to its dispensing are used frequently in the Scriptures. They refer to the Holy Spirit and His coming upon and ministry to and through believers.

The word "pour" brought the image of rain or a heavy shower of rain to the mind of the Jewish listener. The word denotes something coming from above and in great abundance. This idea of abundance is illustrated in the extent of this outpouring—to _all flesh_. Therefore the figure of an abundant rain shower is used to describe the outpouring of the Spirit.

This symbolism of water being poured out carries with it the effects of refreshment and growth. As the showers of the seasonal rain water the earth, the prophet Hosea pictures Jehovah coming to Israel with His ministries of healing and spiritual revival (Hosea 6:3).

In Matthew 3:11, John the Baptist refers to the outpouring of the Holy Spirit as being "baptized" while Luke, the author of Acts, refers to the same experience as being "filled." This is not a contradiction. Actually each word provides a view of the experience from a different vantage point.

The receiving of the Holy Spirit is pictured as a baptism, an immersion under the wave of the divine Spirit as He surges into and over the soul. Consequently the whole being is saturated with the all-pervading, refreshing presence of God.

The word "filled" is used to communicate that the Spirit was not a wind that blew through those who received or a filling that leaked out as through a sieve. They were so full they overflowed through the outlet of speaking with tongues. There was no part of their nature that was not pervaded by the Spirit. Their intellect was enlightened to know the truths of the Spirit. Their affections were purified and infused with desire for heavenly things. Their will was strengthened to obey the desires of the Holy Spirit.

There are many fine Christian people who believe that all Christians are baptized in the Spirit when they are born again. The teaching of Scripture is that the baptism in the Spirit is subsequent to the experience of regeneration, although it may be received simultaneously with the new birth.

Regeneration is a spiritual crisis by which a soul is renewed by the Spirit of God and a new nature is imparted. It reveals a new and divine life, or the production of a new thing. It is a new birth from above.

16. Read the following passages and list what each says about regeneration.

2 Corinthians 5:17 _____

_____

Ephesians 2:1,4 _____

_____

2 Peter 1:4 _____

_____

The baptism in the Holy Spirit is that act of God by which the Holy Spirit comes upon and fills the waiting believer. It is the coming of the Holy Spirit in His own right to fill and possess the child of God. He comes to bring His varied ministries according to His sovereign will. He empowers the believer to be a witness for the gospel of Jesus Christ, through a consistent lifestyle and anointed lips. The distinction between regeneration and the baptism in the Holy Spirit can be illustrated with a few observations.

17. Read Acts 2:4; 8:12-17; 9:17-20; 19:1-7. How do these passages answer the question of when the baptism in the Holy Spirit (or being filled with the Spirit) transpires in a believer's life?

_____

_____

_____

The disciples of Jesus had confessed Him to be the Christ, the Son of the living God (Matthew 16:16; John 6:68,69). Jesus had pronounced them clean with the exception of Judas (John 15:3; 13:10,11). He declared their names were written in heaven (Luke 10:20). He breathed on them with resurrection power (John 20:22). And yet they were commanded to tarry in Jerusalem to receive the baptism in the Holy Spirit (Luke 24:49). They had already received the Spirit in measure, yet they still needed to be baptized in the Holy Spirit.

The Samaritan converts heard the preaching of Philip, responded, believed the message and were baptized. Undoubtedly they had been regenerated by the Holy

Spirit for there was no other way. But they later received the baptism in the Holy Spirit when the apostles came down from Jerusalem and laid hands upon them.

The revelation to Saul on the road to Damascus brought from him the acknowledgment of the Lordship of Jesus. He acknowledged Jesus as Lord and surrendered his life to Him. Upon Saul's arrival in Damascus, Ananias was sent to him and addressing him as "Brother Saul," laid his hands upon him. Saul was delivered of his blindness and was filled with the Holy Spirit.

Acts 19 records the disciples at Ephesus who had been baptized into John's baptism, and were asked by Paul if they had received the Holy Spirit since they believed. What is the significance of Paul's question? If all disciples receive this experience of the Holy Spirit when they believe, why did Paul ask these disciples if they had done so? His question implies that it is possible to believe without receiving the fullness of the Holy Spirit. In the words of A. J. Gordon, "This passage (Acts 19:2) seems decisive as showing that one may be a disciple without having entered into possession of the Spirit as God's gift to believers."

There are many ministries of the Holy Spirit when He enters the believer in His fullness. The basic function of the Holy Spirit is to exalt Christ, to direct attention to Him, and provide a witness unto Him. There are a number of ways by which this is accomplished.

18. Study the following Scripture passages and note some of the ministries of the Holy Spirit.

Romans 8:2 _____

_____

_____

Galatians 5:22 _____

_____

_____

1 John 2:27 _____

_____

_____

SUMMARY

Since God's purposes are accomplished through the power of the Holy Spirit rather than through man (Zechariah 4:6), it is obvious we need the fullness of power and equipment for that development and service. This is provided in the baptism in the Holy Spirit. Our effectiveness as Christians is greatly enhanced by desiring and seeking all that God has to bless us with.

If you have not received this Spirit baptism, repent of your sins, draw close to God and ask Him to pour out His Spirit on you today.

LET'S REVIEW

1. What conditions does Joel's prophecy place on the outpouring of the Holy Spirit?

_____

_____

_____

2. Compare and contrast John's baptism and the baptism Jesus gives.

_____

_____

_____

3. State several noteworthy facts concerning the outpouring of the Spirit at Pentecost.

_____

_____

_____

4. What threefold covenant is seen in Acts 2:38,39?

_____

_____

_____

5. Discuss the relationship between salvation and the baptism in the Holy Spirit.

_____

_____

_____

_____

THE INITIAL EVIDENCE

Most Christians recognize the place of the Holy Spirit in the believer's life and will acknowledge the biblical experience identified as the baptism in the Spirit. But there is difference of opinion, however, as to what time of history this blessing is for and the initial evidence that a person has received this Baptism.

The Book of Acts records the first occurrence of individuals being baptized in the Holy Spirit. It is important to turn there to learn from the historical occurrences regarding the issues of initial evidence and its importance in the life of all believers.

IS SPEAKING IN TONGUES STILL VALID TODAY?

On the Day of Pentecost, people recognized that something supernatural had occurred when they heard individuals speaking in languages that they had never learned. This initial physical evidence continues to signal the baptism in the Holy Spirit today.

When the unusual phenomenon of speaking with other tongues occurred on the Day of Pentecost, many wondered what was going on.

✎ 1. There were a variety of reactions by those who first heard Christians speaking in languages they did not know. Read Acts 2:5-13 and record the reactions recorded in that passage below.

_____

_____

_____

Just as men discredited, mocked, and denied the manifestation of the mighty all-pervading Spirit on the Day of Pentecost, there are those today who do the same. The point of contention in most cases centers around the experience of speaking in tongues.

There are genuine evangelical Christian leaders who argue that this modern recurrence of tongues is Satan's effort to deceive honest, hungry, seeking souls and to impose a counterfeit upon them. They even attribute the phenomenon of tongues to the devil.

✎ 2. Read Acts 1:4-8. In what ways does Jesus endorse the baptism in the Holy Spirit and the initial physical evidence of speaking in tongues?

_____

_____

_____

The baptism in the Spirit, witnessed by speaking with other tongues, ascribes to Jesus His highest place as the Son of God. It exalts Him above every name that is named, and makes Him vividly real to the recipient of that experience. This experience fills the heart of the baptized one with a deep love for Christ and His Word, it inspires with an intense evangelistic zeal, and infuses a desire for holy living. This is the heartfelt testimony of those who have had this experience. Are we to believe that Satan is interested in producing these results? Certainly not. He would be fighting against himself.

For many centuries eminent scholars of Christendom believed speaking in tongues was only for the apostolic period. They advanced the teaching that supernatural signs and gifts recorded in the New Testament were given to affirm the deity of the Lord Jesus, and to authenticate the disciples and their message. Signs and gifts were given to equip the Church against her foes in the days of her establishment.

The one Scripture which seems to support the cessation of tongues is 1 Corinthians 13:8. Verse 8 shows the contrast between love as imperishable and spiritual gifts as impermanent. They will pass away and no longer be needed, but the question is when will this occur?

3. Read 1 Corinthians 13:9,10. When does Paul say tongues, prophecy, and knowledge will no longer exist?

_____

_____

_____

The above passage refers to the future age, when our Lord shall return. Then spiritual gifts and our fragmentary knowledge shall be superseded by a face-to-face revelation of Him who embraces all wisdom and knowledge, and in whom we shall be complete.

Others have rejected speaking in tongues because it has not been a common occurrence throughout Church history.

Although not a day-to-day event until the turn of the 20th century, speaking with other tongues has recurred in every era of Church history, especially during Christian revivals.

The apostolic and post-apostolic fathers of the Church—Irenaeus, Tertullian, Augustine, and others—speak of *glossolalia* (speaking in unknown languages) and the prophetic gift. John Chrysostom, the golden-mouthed preacher and pastor of the church at Constantinople stated, "Whoever was baptized in apostolic days, he straightway spake with tongues." Martin Luther and Francis Xavier are reported by reliable authority to have spoken in tongues. Among the Jansenists and early Quakers, the converts of Wesley and Whitefield, the persecuted Protestants of the Cévennes in France, and the Irvingites, the phenomenon of tongues was present. It also characterized some of the revival meetings of Dwight L. Moody.

4. How may the words spoken by Peter in Acts 2:17 help explain why tongues are such a common occurrence around the world today?

_____

_____

_____

_____

There are some who refuse to label speaking in tongues as satanic yet belittle their importance for contemporary Christians. These individuals would argue that the great apostle Paul himself taught that tongues were a type of spiritual nuisance.

✎ 5. How do Paul's words recorded in 1 Corinthians 14:18 refute the argument that Paul found speaking in tongues distasteful?

_____

_____

_____

_____

It is important for us to understand that the spiritual language referred to by Paul in 1 Corinthians has a different function from the tongues which evidence the baptism in the Holy Spirit. In this study we will limit our focus to the latter phenomena. In any case, the Bible is clear that speaking in tongues is a biblical experience.

✎ 6. Read Hebrews 13:8. How does this verse help validate the occurrences of speaking in tongues today?

_____

_____

_____

_____

IS THERE A BIBLICAL PATTERN?

As noted before, the logical place to look for proof relative to the evidence of receiving the baptism in the Holy Spirit is the Book of Acts. The Book of Acts is not concerned so much with teaching about the Baptism as it is with demonstrating its effect on the life of believers.

The coming of the Holy Spirit on the Day of Pentecost was an antitype or New Testament reflection of the Old Testament _Feast of Weeks_ or _day of the firstfruits_ of the harvest, a day of thanksgiving.

✎ 7. Read Leviticus 23:15-21. Understanding that the Day of Pentecost occurred 50 days after the Passover sabbath, why would people naturally associate the outpouring of the Spirit with the Feast of Weeks?

_____

_____

_____

_____

8. Who was baptized in the Holy Spirit at the initial outpouring according to Acts 1:12-15; 2:4,14,15?

_____

_____

_____

On that momentous day the Spirit fell not only upon the 12 apostles, as some Bible teachers would insist, but upon *all* of those who made up the company of Acts 1.

9. Read John 7:37-39. To whom did Jesus make this promise?

_____

_____

10. Read Acts 10:9-16,19-23,28,46; 11:15-18. How did the events recorded in these passages open the door for the promise of Jesus to become a reality?

_____

_____

_____

_____

What happened at Caesarea, in the demonstration of the Spirit, marked the first outpouring of the Holy Spirit upon the Gentiles. When Peter had preached Jesus as Savior, crucified, resurrected, and the Messiah of prophecy, he and his six Jewish companions were *astonished* to hear these hungry, receptive Gentiles speak with tongues, and magnify God. It is therefore a matter of record that Peter and his comrades recognized tongues as the evidence that the Gentiles received the gift of the Holy Spirit. They later reported this at Jerusalem.

11. Acts 8:4-19 records the events surrounding the baptism in the Holy Spirit as received by the Samaritan believers. Although speaking in tongues is not mentioned specifically here, what indications exist that would make one believe that some type of initial physical evidence occurred?

_____

_____

_____

_____

The preceding incident is out of chronological order for special consideration, because any direct mention of tongues is absent. This fact would seem to contradict the position that *glossolalia* is the initial evidence of the baptism in the Holy Spirit. Despite the absence of the mention of tongues, there is strong evidence this very phenomenon proved the Samaritan believers received the Spirit.

Philip had been preaching to them about Christ, the people had given heed to his message, the message had been confirmed by supernatural signs, "and there was great joy in that city" (Acts 8:8). The new believers were baptized in water. But they had not experienced the baptism in the Spirit. When Peter and John came to them and they received the Baptism, the words used to describe it are very similar to the words describing the experience at Caesarea. What outward sign was evident to Simon and others that the Holy Spirit had fallen? The only previous means of identifying the baptism in the Holy Spirit was speaking in tongues so it would be logical to believe that once again, this phenomenon confirmed the experience.

Matthew Henry, Adam Clarke, Albert Barnes, Alexander Maclaren, and Dr. Henry Alford are but a few scholarly expositors who have gone on record stating they believe the Samaritans spoke in tongues upon receiving the Holy Spirit.

12. Read Acts 19:1-7. Briefly describe the events that transpired when the Ephesian Christians were baptized in the Holy Spirit.

_____

_____

_____

_____

_____

13. Paul himself was baptized in the Holy Spirit. This event is recorded in Acts 9:17-19. What occurred?

_____

_____

_____

_____

_____

It is clear that Paul received the Holy Spirit after his conversion and acknowledgement of the sovereignty of Jesus. Even though only the deliverance from his blindness is specifically mentioned, the commission of Ananias to Paul would not have been completely fulfilled had he not also been filled with the Holy Spirit (Acts 9:17). That Paul did receive the Holy Spirit according to the Pentecostal pattern is attested by his words to the church at Corinth (1 Corinthians 14:18).

IS THERE MORE THAN ONE TYPE OF SPIRITUAL LANGUAGE?

There are inherent similarities in nature between tongues evidencing the Baptism and tongues described as the *gift of tongues* in Paul's First Epistle to the Corinthians. Carl Brumback in his book *What Meaneth This?* outlines the following similarities:

* **The same organs of speech are employed.**
* **The mind is quiescent with respect to the actual exercise of speaking with tongues.**
* **In each form the tongues are the expression of the human spirit under the inspiration of the Holy Spirit.**
* **The miraculous element is present in both.**
* **Both phases are a form of prophecy.**
* **Both are used to praise and magnify God.**

The Scriptures are clear that while there is a similarity between these two manifestations of *glossolalia*, there is a difference in purpose and use. When individuals were initially baptized in the Holy Spirit, tongues were always present as the initial physical evidence to both the individual being baptized and others present. No interpretation was given in those instances because the purpose for the tongues had been accomplished. The sign had been recognized. There is no indication any Early Church leaders involved with these outpourings expected interpretations for the others, or that they saw this as the imparting of a *gift of the Spirit*. First Corinthians 12 to 14, on the other hand, deals solely with information about and rules governing the use of the gifts of the Spirit, including the gifts of tongues and interpretation. We see here the *gift of tongues* has just two purposes: the edification of the individual and those who are present. This is why the *gift of interpretation* is mentioned in conjunction with tongues. As we will see in a later study, after the initial infilling of the Holy Spirit (including the first time of speaking in tongues), we are to continue to live in the fullness of this anointing, including edifying ourselves or others with praying in tongues.

There is a clear distinction between the operation and purpose of evidential tongues and gift tongues.

14. According to 1 Corinthians 12:7-31, not all receive the spiritual gift of speaking in tongues. Why is this gift limited in its distribution?

_____

_____

_____

_____

_____

It is interesting that while not all have the gift of speaking in tongues, all who were baptized in the Holy Spirit in the Early Church spoke in tongues.

✎ 15. List the restrictions placed on public speaking in tongues as outlined in 1 Corinthians 14:26-33.

_____

_____

_____

_____

_____

✎ 16. Why were each of these restrictions imposed?

_____

_____

_____

_____

_____

At Pentecost *all* 120 spoke with other tongues at one time. At Caesarea there was simultaneous *glossolalia*, proven by the pronoun *them*. At Ephesus 12 men spoke with tongues in one meeting and not in sequence! "If all speaking with tongues is the gift, then all these believers, the apostles included, were out of order. How are we to explain this contradiction between apostolic instruction and practice, unless we distinguish between the two phases of tongues? Certainly, the Holy Spirit would not inspire and give utterance in Acts to that which He afterwards condemns in Corinthians!"—Carl Brumback.

SUMMARY

The Bible is clear that speaking with other tongues is the initial physical evidence of the baptism in the Holy Spirit. This being the case, it must be remembered that this does not imply that one should seek for an experience of speaking with tongues primarily. The seeking believer should have as his or her goal to be filled with the Spirit. In faith he or she should plead his or her case before the Supplier of the Baptism—the glorified Christ—and should expect that Baptism to be accompanied by speaking with other tongues. Christ himself promised that such a supernatural sign would follow the faith of the believer (Mark 16:17).

Every believer who has not yet received the Baptism is to *ask, seek, and knock,* and expect to *receive, find, and enter*!

LET'S REVIEW

✎ 1. How do the accounts recorded in the Book of Acts demonstrate that speaking in tongues is the initial physical evidence of the baptism in the Holy Spirit?

_____

_____

_____

✎ 2. How can the argument that this phenomenon was exclusively for the apostolic period be refuted biblically?

_____

_____

_____

✎ 3. How would you respond to someone who said Paul discredited the practice of speaking in tongues? Provide biblical evidence.

_____

_____

_____

✎ 4. Explain the difference between speaking in tongues as the initial evidence of the baptism in the Spirit and the spiritual gift of speaking in tongues.

_____

_____

_____

✎ 5. List questions which you still have regarding the practice and purpose of speaking in tongues.

_____

_____

_____

STUDY 5

HOW TO RECEIVE THE BAPTISM

L earning about the Holy Spirit is exciting. But some may ask questions such as, "Is this experience for me?"; "How may I receive it?"; "What must I do to receive it?"

The baptism in the Holy Spirit is the privilege of every believer, and each one should receive this wonderful experience. The identical experience received by believers in the Early Church is promised to all Christians.

The gift of the Holy Spirit has been purchased for us by Christ, and is now available by grace through faith. The only condition which must be met before individuals can receive is salvation through faith in the atonement of Christ. There are, however, certain fundamental truths and principles that will help the believer who seeks the baptism in the Holy Spirit.

PREPARING TO RECEIVE

Some people teach that there are specific formulas which must be followed when one seeks the baptism in the Holy Spirit. These formulas often entail specific sounds to be made, postures to hold, or places to be. These formulas find no basis in Scripture. Biblical examples of people who were baptized in the Holy Spirit show they did not conjure up the Holy Spirit. Rather, they simply opened themselves to this spiritual reality.

✎ 1. Compare and contrast the conditions that surrounded those who were baptized in the Holy Spirit on the Day of Pentecost (Acts 2:1-4) with Paul's experience recorded in Acts 9:10-19. If there was a formula used in either situation regarding posture, place, or activity, record it below.

_____

_____

_____

_____

_____

Although no formula exists, a clean heart is a prerequisite to receiving the Baptism. The baptism in the Holy Spirit is given only to those whose hearts have been cleansed by the precious blood of Christ. The Holy Spirit cannot come to dwell in a temple which is unclean.

A seeking heart is important in receiving anything from God. The Bible gives many examples of spiritual accomplishments that are a direct result of seeking by God's people (2 Chronicles 7:14; Psalm 34:10; Jeremiah 29:10-14; Matthew 7:8; and Luke 12:31).

✎ 2. What response was given to an individual who sought the baptism in the Holy Spirit from a wrong motive? (Acts 8:14-24).

_____

_____

_____

_____

How does one seek the baptism in the Holy Spirit? In the early days of the modern Pentecostal movement, many pointed to the extended prayer meeting which preceded the Day of Pentecost and taught that waiting or "tarrying" before the Lord brought spiritual results. Prayer meetings would often extend into the early morning hours, even lasting through the night occasionally. Many were baptized in the Spirit as a result of these prolonged times of prayer.

One of the key ingredients in the process of "tarrying" is the personal and spiritual adjustments made as a result of time spent in the presence of God. Protracted waiting is not imperative to accomplish this, for adjustment can be made quickly by yielding to God. Such waiting may be profitable while a deep work of sanctification is being accomplished in the soul. The need to "tarry" is proportional to an individual's willingness to submit to the corrective instructions of God.

✎ 3. Read each of the following passages and record the requirements made by God and results which He promises to those who obey.

2 Chronicles 7:14 _____

_____

_____

Psalm 34:10 _____

_____

_____

Jeremiah 29:10-14 _____

_____

_____

Matthew 7:7,8 _____

_____

_____

Luke 12:31 _____

_____

_____

The seeker should evidence his or her earnest desire to be filled. A listless, passive attitude will never elicit a response from God. Jesus showed the need of a *never give up* attitude in Luke 11:1-13. The passage is more than a promise-encouraging prayer. It is a declaration of the condition of our receiving any good gift from God. There is a treasure-house full of His grace.

God limited himself in the provision of these promises by certain principles inherent in His creation of us. Prayer (asking, seeking, knocking) recognizes the sovereign freedom of the human will. God can move on a hardened heart, but chooses not to push himself on His creation.

Prayer also indicates some sympathy on the part of the person praying for God's will and purposes. It manifests a desire to cooperate with God in carrying out these purposes.

✎ **4. To whom does God give the Holy Spirit according to Acts 5:32?**

_____

_____

_____

Obedience and submission to the will of God are necessary conditions to receiving from Him. He is sovereign. His will is supreme. He is Lord and we are His servants. He commands; we must obey—not by compulsion, but in glad, joyous response, for His will is good, pleasing, and perfect. God must be sure He is bestowing this precious gift upon one who has renounced all claims to himself and his own plans and ways and is truly devoted to God.

✎ **5. Read Romans 12:1,2. If you don't have this passage committed to memory, do it now, and let it be a daily reminder of your dedication to God. Make a list of areas of your life in which you have been conforming to the world. Next, write a prayer of confession, including your request for God's help in these areas of weakness.**

_____

_____

_____

_____

_____

_____

_____

_____

_____

_____

_____

_____

_____

_____

_____

Faith in God and His promises is essential to receiving all that the Holy Spirit wants to do for us. Faith, if it is to be effective in accomplishing desired results, must have assurance.

✎ 6. Read Hebrews 11:1 and paraphrase it below.

_____

_____

_____

_____

_____

_____

_____

Hebrews 11:1 may not be so much a definition as a description of a state of the soul which results from faith. Note the phrases *being sure of* and *certain of*. According to Dr. Edgar Goodspeed, in his Bible translation, "Faith means the assurance of what we hope for: it is our conviction about things that we cannot see"; or Weymouth's narrative, "Now faith is a well-grounded assurance of that of which we hope, and a conviction of the reality of things we do not see." How do we get this assurance and conviction of faith? From His promise or divine Word.

✎ 7. Read Luke 11:13. What assurance does this passage give to those who wish to be baptized in the Holy Spirit?

_____

_____

_____

_____

We have learned in Hebrews 11:1 that we can count on God's promises even though they have yet to occur. Luke 11:13 affirms the fact that God wishes to baptize us in the Holy Spirit. The logical extension of these two passages for those who have not been baptized is to anticipate its reality in our lives.

The following scenario illustrates this point. The day after Christmas as a little boy was playing beneath the tree with his new toys, a neighbor came by.

"Well, Johnny," she asked, "how many Christmas presents did you receive yesterday?"

"Five," he replied quickly.

Johnny's mother, thinking he had miscounted, turned to him and said, "Johnny, didn't you receive only four presents?"

"No, Mama, I received five," was his reaffirmation.

"How's that? You have only four there."

"But, Mama," he insisted, "Grandma gave me a scooter."

"But you haven't received the scooter," his mother replied.

"Yes, but I know the scooter is coming, because Grandma said she would send it."

Sure enough, the next day Johnny received a note from his grandmother in another city saying she was initially unable to find the scooter, but to be on the look-out for it in a few days.

True to the grandmother's word, the scooter arrived. Johnny turned to his mother as they opened the package and said, "Mama, didn't I tell you the other day that I received five Christmas presents?"

Johnny was right. And the same principle applies in seeking the baptism in the Holy Spirit, or any other blessing God has promised. He is true to His Word. Believe He hears you and be on the lookout, as Johnny was, until the gift arrives.

This attitude of trustful waiting should be accompanied by praise. Praise or thanksgiving manifests a pre-acknowledgment of God's faithfulness to give His blessing, and demonstrates an expectation that it will be received.

What shall we praise our Lord for? Everything! All that we have and are is the result of His goodness and grace. Praise Him for who He is. Praise Him for a divine love that caused Him to die for us, affording us a wonderful salvation. Thank Him for the witness already received that we are His children. Praise Him in advance and in anticipation of receiving the Baptism which we seek. What we ask for with an attitude of praise, we shall receive.

HOW MAY WE HELP THE SEEKER

It is clear that God used humans in the Early Church to help others receive the baptism in the Holy Spirit. This was so at Samaria when Peter and John laid their hands upon the newly saved Samaritan believers (Acts 8:14,17). This same phenomenon holds true today. We may know of someone the Lord seems to especially use in praying for others to receive the Baptism.

8. Although God uses people to help individuals receive the baptism in the Holy Spirit, who is the Baptizer in the Holy Spirit? (Matthew 3:11; John 15:26; 16:7).

_____

_____

_____

_____

_____

_____

_____

9. What commands are Christians given in Ephesians 6:18?

_____

_____

_____

Whatever our brothers and sisters in the Lord need, it is our privilege to exercise the ministry of intercession in their behalf. In the case of the seeker for the Baptism, we may stand with him or her in prayer that he may quickly be reconciled to God, if necessary.

We may praise the Lord with him and create an atmosphere of faith. The Scripture says that God inhabits the praises of His people (Psalm 22:3, KJV). He delights to manifest His presence where He is honored and worshiped. Our adversary, Satan, may attempt to inject unbelief, doubt, and fear to hinder our receiving from God. But in such an atmosphere of praise, Satan will find it impossible to stay. He cannot breathe there. Praise creates a stifling atmosphere for Satan.

Overly zealous individuals have hindered seekers by manipulation, contrary to any divine instruction in the Word. When the Spirit comes upon the seeker, those trying to help attempt to instruct the seeker by saying: "Now, let the Holy Ghost have His way, brother"; "That's it, just yield to the Lord"; "Let Him have your tongue," etc., often distract and sometimes hinder the seeker's quest.

Personal experience has proven this to be the case. When personally seeking for the baptism in the Holy Spirit, two good sisters, one on each side, surrounded me. The instructions were so repetitious I could not get my mind upon the Lord and had to pray in my own heart, "Lord, please deliver me from these two sisters!"

The mighty, omnipotent Third Person of the Trinity, who in the Baptism is touching one of God's children, is not to be belittled by human efforts. A misguided Pentecostal leader in Scotland got an idea some years back. He reasoned that since we overcome _by the blood of the Lamb,_ and since Satan opposes the seeker of the Baptism, pleading _the blood_ against Satan by repeating the word _blood_ would defeat the enemy. Seekers were counseled to do this. This procedure led to rapidly repeating the word _blood_ until a seeker's tongue became tangled and it seemed like speaking with tongues.

The word _blood_ in itself is no mystic key that opens the door to God's blessings, or produces extraordinary effects, even when spoken in rapid repetition.

Likewise, repetition of phrases or words of praise such as _Glory to God,_ or _Hallelujah,_ etc.—has no virtue in itself. Praise must come from deep within the soul to reach the ear and heart of God. When it is done in faith, the answer is sure to come.

SUMMARY

What infinite, glorious love that God should reconcile sinners to himself by the death of His Son. Then, that He should make that relationship so real by the witness of the Spirit, and also fill or baptize in that same Spirit.

If you have not taken full advantage of this love, God's promises are for you. Ask your Heavenly Father to reveal any areas in your life that are hindering your Baptism, repent, and then open yourself to the life-changing baptism in the Holy Spirit.

LET'S REVIEW

1. What role do posture, time, and place have when seeking to receive the baptism in the Holy Spirit? Explain.

_____

_____

_____

_____

2. How should a person prepare to be baptized in the Holy Spirit?

_____

_____

_____

_____

3. What role do believers have in helping individuals become baptized in the Holy Spirit?

_____

_____

_____

_____

_____

4. What actions should be avoided when helping an individual become baptized in the Holy Spirit?

_____

_____

_____

_____

STUDY 6

IS THERE MORE?

Many misinformed believers have received a false impression that the baptism in the Holy Spirit is a climactic experience, a final goal to be reached. This wrong concept has led some to believe the initial experience of being baptized in the Holy Spirit is sufficient in itself. Actually the baptism in the Holy Spirit is an introduction to the Spirit-filled life. It is the doorway into an ever-increasing awareness of the loveliness and wonders of our incomparable Christ. As we walk by the Spirit in fellowship with Him, we are strengthened to maintain the anointing we have received.

WHAT DOES IT MEAN TO BE "SPIRIT-FILLED"?

1. Read Ephesians 5:18. Physical drunkenness results in counterfeit emotions often lumped together under the heading of "having a good time." Why do you think Paul used physical drunkenness as a launching pad to encourage Christians to be filled with the Spirit?

_____

_____

_____

_____

In order to correctly evaluate the Spirit-filled life and to stimulate a desire to be filled with the Spirit, let us look at the lives of several Spirit-filled men from God's Word. Their lives can serve as powerful examples of the possibilities of living in the Spirit.

2. Read Acts 3:1 to 5:42. Summarize the effect of the Holy Spirit on the lives and ministries of Peter, John, and various other church leaders. Cite specific examples.

_____

_____

_____

_____

3. According to Acts 4:33, what is the purpose of a Spirit-filled life?

_____

_____

_____

4. Read John 7:37-39. How can a person be continually filled with the Spirit to the point of overflowing?

_____

_____

_____

Stephen was one of the first deacons chosen in the Early Church.

✎ 5. According to Acts 6:3, what qualification did the Early Church determine was necessary to function in the role of a spiritual servant?

_____

_____

_____

While holding an undistinguished office, he was considered a mighty man of God, a fearless apologist of the faith and one through whom great wonders and miracles were performed among the people.

Here is encouragement to the humblest believer that he may accomplish great things for God.

✎ 6. Read Stephen's sermon preached before the Sanhedrin in Acts 7:1-60. Based on this sermon and his reactions, evaluate Stephen in the following categories. List verses where these characteristics are demonstrated.

Bold _____

_____

_____

_____

_____

Uncompromising _____

_____

_____

_____

Humble _____

_____

_____

_____

_____

Being full of the Holy Spirit brought Stephen so intimately in touch with God he was given a glimpse of heaven and of Jesus himself (Acts 7:55). This was in preparation for Stephen's immediate martyrdom.

7. Read Acts 13:6-12. What evidence of the Holy Spirit's ongoing power at work in the life of the apostle Paul is recorded there?

_____

_____

_____

Paul illustrates the power of a Spirit-filled life in his dealing with Elymas, the sorcerer on the island of Cyprus. This proves that when one is filled with the Spirit, he is ready for any emergency.

8. Barnabas was another church leader who demonstrated a Spirit-filled life. Read Acts 11:23,24 and record the author's description of Barnabas.

_____

_____

_____

_____

Through Barnabas' ministry a great number of people were saved, and he became the associate of Paul in pioneer ministry.

9. According to Ephesians 5:18-20, what is a natural by-product of being Spirit-filled?

_____

_____

_____

HOW DO YOU STAY FILLED?

It is not possible for Christians to maintain the same spiritual level. There are mysterious risings and fallings of the spiritual and mental barometer due to the storms of life. The soul has its periods of high and low pressure. We are subjected to many influences over which we have no control.

But there is one impulse which the Holy Spirit stimulates and that is singing to the Lord. There are many instances in the Word where the expression *sing unto the Lord,* or like terms, is used to point to the importance songs have in the life of the saint of God. David contributed to our spiritual inspiration in the songs he penned, some of which we now know as the Psalms.

A melodious heart then, is a sign of a Spirit-filled person. Saints of God are privileged to join with all nature in singing unto the Lord (not just singing songs). Singing drives dull thoughts away. It routs the enemy as it infuses courage. It refreshes and stimulates the physical man. It glorifies God. It lightens and exhilarates the soul.

✎ 10. Look up the following verses and record each situation in which singing was used.

Matthew 26:30 _____

_____

_____

Acts 16:25 _____

_____

_____

Thomas Fuller, noted for his quaintness as well as for the wisdom of his remarks, had a defective voice; but he did not refuse to praise on this account. "Lord," he said, "my voice by nature is harsh and untunable, and it is vain to lavish any art to better it. Can my singing of psalms be pleasing to Thine ears, which is unpleasant to my own? Yet, though I cannot chant with the nightingale, or chirp with the blackbird, I had rather chatter with the swallow than be altogether silent. Now what my music wants in sweetness, let it have in sense. Yea, Lord, create in me a new heart, therein to make melody, and I will be contented with my old voice, until in due time, being admitted into the choir of heaven, I shall have another voice more harmonious bestowed upon me." So let it be with us. Let us ever sing in the same spirit and in the same joy and hope.

Another characteristic of a Spirit-filled believer is a thankful heart. Thankfulness is that attitude which acknowledges all blessings. A grateful heart retains the impression of past mercies. Gratitude adequately evaluates God's blessings. Thanksgiving is a true acknowledgement of respect for our Heavenly Father and the fact we are dependent on Him.

✎ 11. Read 1 Corinthians 4:7. How does this information help us focus our thankfulness toward God?

_____

_____

_____

_____

The grateful heart is to be thankful *for all things*—the things we know are good, those which we deem good, and even for those things that do not seem to be good at all.

✎ **12. Look up Romans 8:28; Hebrews 13:15; and 1 Peter 2:5 and summarize what these verses say concerning thanksgiving.**

_____

_____

_____

_____

_____

Our thanksgiving is to be in the name of our Lord Jesus Christ. It is His intercession on our behalf that renders us acceptable in the Beloved, and by the incense of His worthiness our thanksgiving is perfumed.

The Spirit-filled heart gives thanks always, the Scripture says.

He provides daily benefits for us. Since this is true, our thanksgiving to God should be expressed not only on the Lord's Day, but during the week. There should be a daily balance of giving thanks that no blessing may fail to be counted.

✎ **13. In Galatians 5:22-26, record the spiritual fruits that should be evident in the Spirit-filled life.**

_____

_____

_____

Love unites us with God; *joy* is thanksgiving and awareness of living in God's infinite goodness; *peace* describes the condition when we are at rest with God, ourselves, and all mankind.

Then there are the fruits which relate to our neighbor, and the first is *patience*. Do we tolerate our neighbors? Are we irritable, vengeful, resentful, malicious? If so, the fruits of the Holy Spirit are not fully manifesting themselves in us. Just as equity is the most delicate form of justice, patience is the most perfect form of charity. The perpetual radiance of a loving heart looks kindly upon our neighbors and does not judge their faults. It also means *perseverance*. This means not showing a tedious spirit in well-doing. It is not giving up and saying, "I have tried to do a good deed, but he is ungrateful, incorrigible, and I will have no more to do with him." Gratefully, our Lord does not deal with us in this manner. Patience means perseverance in doing good. *Kindness* means giving preference, the absence of resentment and suppressing unkind thoughts. Next comes *goodness*. As a fountain pours out pure water, so the good heart continually pours out goodness that is reproduced in others. *Faithfulness* means veracity, so that a man's word is as good as an oath.

Then there are certain fruits which reference our own lives. They are, first, *gentleness* (meekness), which is both intrinsic and external. Gentleness of conduct, gentleness of dress and appearance, a sensitive regard for others, is due from us to them. This keeps us from interfering with their individual rights. *Self-control* or temperance, means repressing passions—the passion of anger, the inclination to pleasure, to receive honor, or wealth. These are the fruits of the Holy Spirit. Every soul in the grace of God should evidence these fruits in their fullness.

14. In light of what you have just read, why do you think Jesus reacted as He did in the story recorded in Matthew 21:18,19?

_____

_____

_____

God's mandate is that all life be nurtured. Sinful man is wasteful. He dissipates his physical energies in sensual pleasures. He wastes vast material resources in war and conflict. In his greed of gain, he wastes the vast resources of nature—the soil, lumber, oil, and mineral wealth.

But while God is a lavish Giver, He hates waste. Consequently He established with Adam in the Garden of Eden the principle of cultivation or nurture.

God put man into the Garden of Eden *to work it and to take care of it* (Genesis 2:15). Man was responsible for the continuance of the ideal state of the Garden.

The spiritual realm is no different. God confers upon us all the good things we need in the ministries of the indwelling Spirit. But He also requires that we cooperate with the Spirit in nurturing and cherishing these divine resources.

The exhortation of Ephesians 5:18, "Be filled with the Spirit," is in the present, passive imperative and may be accurately translated, "Be being filled with the Spirit." This indicates there should be a continuous process or experience of being kept filled, because of a constant connection with the source of supply.

The channel through which the Spirit must work is human and frail. Sometimes that channel becomes clogged with failure and sin and must come to the Lord in confession and supplication for cleansing.

Thus, we are exhorted to wait upon the Lord.

15. What does Isaiah 40:31 tell us about the benefit of waiting on the Lord?

_____

_____

_____

_____

What does it mean to *wait upon God*? When the Word speaks of waiting upon God it means something quite different from doing nothing. If we think waiting is not activity, we miss the thought entirely.

16. What kind of action is described in the last part of Psalm 123:2?

_____

_____

_____

The waiting of the servant and the maiden in the passage represents being in the presence of their master or mistress, alert to carry out their orders.

What are the elements involved in waiting upon God?

We wait upon God when we pray. He will bless us in our prayers, if we exhibit a true heart and an attitude of expectant dependency.

We wait upon God when we purpose to obey Him, as the servant does his master.

We wait upon God when we seek to do His will and discover He will empower us to fulfill His commands.

We wait upon God when we do a kindly deed, express an encouraging word, give a cup of cold water to the thirsty, serve for Jesus' sake, or perform any menial service for His glory. We must be willing to minister these deeds rather than something which brings public recognition and acclaim.

We wait upon God as we love Him. Jacob waited for Rachel 7 years and labored on without payment by his uncle. These years seemed but a few days due to his great love for her. Others would have tired of waiting, but he remained strong. Unless we love God, any waiting upon Him is shallow.

Those who wait upon God are renewed, refreshed, and are refilled with His Spirit, because it is there He reveals himself.

17. According to James 4:8, what will God do if we come to Him?

_____

_____

_____

SUMMARY

The exciting news of Scripture reveals that the baptism in the Holy Spirit is just the start of the Christian's adventure into the "Spirit-filled" world. Those who become satisfied with the initial experience without seeking additional "fillings" miss out on much that God has to offer.

The Bible offers many examples of individuals who had their weaknesses turned into strengths as a result of the Spirit. The Spirit enabled individuals who faced great trials to be victorious.

That same resource is available to Christians today. We must be willing to create an atmosphere of thanksgiving, be willing to confront sin in our lives, and wait upon God to fill us with His Spirit daily so that we can minister effectively to others in His strength.

LET'S REVIEW

✏️ 1. How did being Spirit-filled impact the lives of the leaders in the Early Church? Provide examples.

_____

_____

_____

✏️ 2. What role does music play in the process of being continually filled with the Spirit?

_____

_____

_____

✏️ 3. List the fruit of the Spirit one can expect to display as a result of being Spirit-filled.

_____

_____

_____

✏️ 4. What role does waiting play in being filled with the Spirit? Explain how one should learn to wait.

_____

_____

_____

✏️ 5. Have you taken opportunity to wait upon God, and receive a fresh anointing of His Spirit? Describe your experience below.

_____

_____

_____

GIFTS OF THE SPIRIT, PART 1

The gifts of the Spirit are an extension of the baptism in the Holy Spirit. They have been made available to the Church for its own edification, to glorify Christ, and to extend the kingdom of God.

It is important that we understand the gifts the Spirit bestows upon us. Before a tool or machine can be used, a workman must know what it is for, how it is constructed, how the various parts are related and controlled, what it is intended to do, and how this can best be accomplished. So it is with these gracious gifts of the Holy Spirit.

In this study, we will examine the first two of the general categories often associated with the spiritual gifts—the revelation gifts and the gifts related to speech.

THE REVELATION GIFTS

The revelation gifts are given by the Spirit to help the individual and congregation understand more fully the mind and heart of God. Three specific manifestations of the revelation gifts are mentioned in Scripture.

Wisdom

The first gift listed in 1 Corinthians 12:8 refers to a "word or message of wisdom." Note this bestowment is not a gift of wisdom in the abstract sense, but of the *word* or *message of wisdom*. It is important because wisdom implies knowledge and is the ability to profitably apply knowledge in a discreet fashion.

1. Read Colossians 2:2,3 and record Christ's relation to wisdom and knowledge.

_____

_____

_____

_____

True wisdom is possessed by God and is resident in Him in infinite, limitless measure. The *word* or *message of wisdom* is a portion of that infinite wisdom of God, which He reveals through one of His Spirit-filled children. It may take a number of forms.

2. Read 1 Corinthians 2. What does Paul state concerning God's wisdom and man's wisdom?

_____

_____

_____

Paul makes a clear distinction between the *wisdom of men* and the *wisdom of God*. He emphasizes that he set aside personal wisdom that he might be a channel for the revelation of the wisdom of God. Paul clearly shows that the *word of wisdom* is distinct from merely abstract wisdom.

3. What wisdom does Paul claim to speak to the church in Corinth? (1 Corinthians 2:6,7,13).

_____

_____

_____

According to Donald Gee: "The use of the gift in these passages is for the opening up of truth concerning the preaching of the Cross, and the things which God hath prepared for them that love Him: and we have no hesitation in affirming that here we have one of the highest and truest uses of the gift revealed.... The gift of the *word of wisdom* when thus used, brought to the heart a revelation of the truth that was intuitive, and yet convincing."

The *word of wisdom* is exemplified in its use as the Holy Spirit's defense against those opposed to the truth of God.

✎ 4. What does Jesus promise to do for His disciples in Luke 12:11,12; 21:14,15?

_____

_____

_____

Our Lord promised His disciples an endowment of heavenly wisdom. Stephen exemplified this endowment in Acts 6:10.

Two occasions are recorded in our Lord's ministry when the manifestation of divine wisdom found expression.

✎ 5. Look up the following passages and describe each instance and Jesus' response to being challenged:

Matthew 21:23-27 _____

_____

Luke 20:20-26 _____

_____

Jesus' answers to His opponents were so wise and astounding that He sent them away confused and ashamed.

The Old Testament records events when *words of wisdom* were given to select people for specific purposes. A few examples include Joseph whom God endowed with wisdom to save a nation, Solomon who governed Israel, and Daniel who was repeatedly given the *word of wisdom* and *revelation* as he stood firm in the face of spiritual opposition.

✎ 6. Read the following Scriptures and summarize how *words of wisdom* from God were used to benefit God's servants and the cause of His kingdom.

Genesis 41:1-40 _____

_____

_____

1 Kings 3:16-28 _____

_____

_____

Daniel 1:17-20; 2:1-49 _____

_____

_____

Knowledge

Knowledge is a prerequisite of wisdom, for wisdom is the application of knowledge to a desired end. Knowledge is accumulation of facts either divinely imparted, or acquired through the intellect. The spiritual gift associated with knowledge is best labeled the *word* or *message of knowledge.* A word is the outward, audible expression of the invisible thought, just as Christ is the Word of God who is the objective, physical expression of God himself.

The *word* or *message of knowledge* is usually demonstrated as a Spirit-inspired utterance (1 Corinthians 12) or through structured teaching (Romans 12:6,7). This *gift* as the *word of knowledge* can be used as a portion of knowledge revealed for a specific crisis in the Church assembly. However, we are not to assume that we can obtain the limitless wealth of knowledge which God possesses. Rather, out of God's limitless store of knowledge, He chooses to reveal through the Spirit-filled believer that *word of knowledge*, which will edify, encourage, or fortify the Church.

Donald Gee feels the office of the teacher has a distinct relation to this spiritual investment. He says: "The gift of the *word of knowledge* lies at the root of the office of the teacher. It is this spiritual gift above all others which the true teacher possesses and exercises in the assemblies. Note particularly, however, that it is a divine gift, and most emphatically does not consist merely in natural powers of analysis, logic, and exposition. It manifests the Holy Spirit operating through the teacher, and the intellectual powers at work are receiving their knowledge by a process of divine illumination." In other words, the *word of knowledge* is an expression of knowledge gained, not through a process of reasoning, but a supernatural revelation of fact through the divine Spirit.

✎ **7. Read Acts 11:27-30 and 21:10,11. How was the *word of knowledge* used in each of these instances and by whom?**

_____

_____

The *gift of knowledge* may also be provided by God to impart knowledge of happenings which are necessary for His people to know for their own enlightenment and protection. The *word of knowledge* functions sometimes through the ministry of prophecy. These *gifts* are not separate and distinct bestowments upon individuals, but are manifested by the Holy Spirit himself through the inspired believer.

8. The following instances of knowledge of persons and happenings illustrate the *word of knowledge.* Describe each situation.

1 Samuel 9:15,16 _____

_____

_____

1 Samuel 10:2 _____

_____

_____

1 Samuel 10:21,22 _____

_____

_____

2 Kings 5:26 _____

_____

_____

2 Kings 6:8-12 _____

_____

_____

John 1:48 _____

_____

_____

John 4:18 _____

_____

_____

John 11:12-14 _____

_____

_____

_____

Discerning Of Spirits

This *gift* is not in display when people claim to uncover others' motives and proceed to expose them under the guise of *discerning of spirits*. It is not keen insight into human nature, which a psychiatrist may possess. It has to do with *discerning of spirits*, not of men in their natural courses of action.

The unseen world of *spirits* is divided into two realms—those presided over by God and ones under the authority of Satan. Archangels, angels, cherubim, and seraphim do the bidding of God, while the evil angels and demons carry out Satan's designs (Ephesians 6:11,12). These two realms are in conflict. "God, the Holy Spirit is the active Commander-in-Chief of God's army. He personally indwells and energizes Spirit-filled believers. A valuable weapon both of defense and offense for them is the gift of the *discerning of spirits*."—Ralph Riggs.

The nature of this *gift* is found in the word *discerning* (Greek—*diakrisis*) meaning "a judging through." The essential thought is to make a distinction or to discriminate. It is a piercing of that which is outward and ensuring that a correct judgment may be based on that insight.

Discernment is an attribute of God encompassing absolute knowledge of all things, the perfect power of "judging through." By this power He is qualified to be the Judge of all the earth.

9. What do the following Scriptures say about God's discernment with us? (1 Chronicles 28:9; Psalm 139:1-24; and Jeremiah 17:10).

_____

_____

_____

_____

_____

The function of *discerning of spirits* is to help the Church encounter the powers of darkness.

10. How is Satan described in Ephesians 2:2?

_____

_____

_____

_____

Satan also possesses the minds and bodies of susceptible unbelievers through evil spirits or demons. He uses them to attack the gospel and attempt to deceive the Christian community.

✎ 11. Read Acts 5:1-4; 8:20-23; 13:6-12; and 16:16-18, then record the instances where Peter and Paul used the gift of *discerning of spirits.*

_____

_____

_____

Peter exposed Simon the sorcerer, discerning the condition of his heart, though outwardly Simon had apparently deceived the other believers. We need discernment today, for many Christians are unaware of the presence of the spiritual realm. This *gift* can reveal to a Spirit-filled body of believers the source of any supernatural manifestation.

✎ 12. What does the Bible say about the need for spiritual discernment in the last days? (2 Thessalonians 2:9; 1 Timothy 4:1; Revelation 13:14).

_____

_____

_____

It is clear from God's Word the end-time will be characterized by a resurgence of the (satanic) supernatural. False doctrines, propagated by seducing demon spirits will be prevalent. The tribulation days will be filled with satanic miracles, and it is possible even before the Rapture, the Church may have to face supernatural events which will deceive many Christians.

The revelation gifts of *wisdom*, *knowledge*, and *discerning of spirits* provide the Church with an avenue of obtaining divine direction for situations which require capacities beyond one's own capabilities.

THE SPEECH GIFTS

The *gifts of revelation* express the mind of God; the *gifts of power* (which we will discuss in the next study) express His might and power; while the *gifts of speech* give expression to the feelings of His infinite heart.

✎ 13. Read 1 Corinthians 14:1-5 and respond below whether one gift is given precedence over any other. Why do you believe this to be true?

_____

_____

_____

Prophecy

Among the gifts, *prophecy* is one which believers are exhorted to eagerly desire. Ralph Riggs has said: "A possible reason for the precedence given this gift is that through its medium, the other best gifts find expression. Wisdom must be voiced or else it remains unused and latent. *Prophecy* is the voice through which wisdom speaks. Faith [to be discussed in the next study] is the word of authority and must be spoken to be effective. *Prophecy* is the voice by which faith speaks. And *prophecy* has a function all its own as well. It is the voice of the Holy Spirit speaking through a divinely inspired, yielded, chosen channel." The Holy Spirit desires and wills to speak for the benefit of the individual believer and of the Church collectively. The *gift of prophecy* provides this channel among Spirit-filled people.

Prophecy is distinct from ordinary preaching, though this too may be anointed by the Holy Spirit. *Prophecy* is preaching, but with a distinct characteristic. *Prophecy* in the scriptural sense means to speak forth the message of God for the immediate occasion, and sometimes, as in the case of Agabus (Acts 11:27-30; 21:10,11), foretelling a future event.

We must distinguish how this *gift* was used in the New Testament Church and in Old Testament times. Samuel, for example, was the recognized spokesman in his day, not only for Jehovah to Israel, but also for the people to Jehovah.

14. In 1 Samuel 3:19-21; 8:21, how was Samuel used by God?

_____

_____

_____

Donald Gee stated: "All this is changed in the new dispensation ushered in at Pentecost. It is now the privilege of all believers to be personally led by the Spirit of God (Romans 8:14); it cannot be too emphatically stated that we need neither prophet nor priest to come between ourselves and the Lord in this present dispensation, and to submit for one moment to such a system is a definite step backwards into bondage."

15. According to Paul in 1 Corinthians 14:3, what function does the *gift of prophecy* play in the ministry of the Church?

_____

_____

_____

_____

Tongues

Pentecostals recognize a distinction between *tongues* as the initial evidence of receiving the baptism in the Spirit and the *gift of tongues*. The former is the normal Christian experience and is for all, but the latter is limited in its distribution.

✎ 16. Look up Acts 2:4,38,39 and 1 Corinthians 12:27-31. What do Luke and Paul say about *initial evidence* and the *gift of tongues?*

_____

_____

_____

The *gift of tongues* is "the power of utterance in languages unknown to the speaker, given to certain individuals in the Church by the Spirit of God, and capable of interpretation by means of an equally supernatural 'gift,' in order that these utterances may thereby become intelligible to the assembly."—Donald Gee.

When the *gift of interpretation* is in operation together with *tongues,* the two are equivalent to *prophecy* (1 Corinthians 14:5).

✎ 17. What does 1 Corinthians 14:14 say about the connection between *tongues* and our spirit?

_____

_____

Interpretation Of Tongues

The *gift of interpretation of tongues* is analogous to interpreting a foreign tongue into a known language of a culture by one who knows both languages. But the spiritual gift is different in its nature and mode of operation from ordinary interpreting. It is a supernatural bestowment of the Holy Spirit. It implies no natural knowledge by the interpreter of the language spoken in tongues. Again Donald Gee helps us here. The interpretation is received, not "by close attention to the words of the one speaking in tongues, but by close concentration in spirit upon the Lord, who alone gives the interpretation. The words are given by revelation, and follow the rules of prophecy and all inspired utterance, coming either by vision, by burden, or by suggestion, just as the Lord may choose."

SUMMARY

Personal possession or selfish use of spiritual gifts is never communicated in Scripture. All *gifts of the spirit*, including abilities, ministries, administration, and spiritual occurrences, are presented as "the manifestation of the Spirit," which is given for the profit or edification of all (1 Corinthians 12:7).

It is thrilling to know that God in His wisdom provided ways by which His presence and power may be manifested in the midst of His people. It is encouraging to know that God has equipped His people for the conflict against principalities and powers. It is blessed to know He provided the abilities for the Church's work of kingdom expansion.

As we come to know the nature and purpose of these *gifts,* we should be inspired to earnestly desire them, pray for them, and to achieve their most blessed and effective operation among God's people.

LET'S REVIEW

1. Define and explain the *word of wisdom.* Give examples of its use.

_____

_____

_____

2. Define and explain the *word of knowledge.* Give examples of its use.

_____

_____

_____

3. Define and explain the function of *discerning of spirits.* Give instances of its operation.

_____

_____

4. Define and explain *prophecy* as a gift of the Spirit.

_____

_____

5. Define and explain *tongues* and *interpretation of tongues.*

_____

_____

_____

6. Based on 1 Corinthians 12 and Romans 12, what is the purpose and distribution of spiritual gifts?

_____

_____

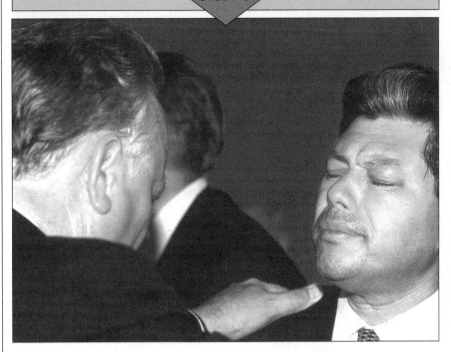

GIFTS OF THE SPIRIT, PART 2

I n the last study, we looked at the three gifts classified as *gifts of revelation* and at three gifts considered *gifts of speech*. In this study, we will look at the final three gifts mentioned in 1 Corinthians 12, additional spiritual gifts mentioned in Romans 12, and the ministry gifts to the Church listed in Ephesians 4.

It is important to remember these gifts are from God. We cannot manufacture them ourselves, nor should we feel superior if the Holy Spirit decides to bestow a gift or gifts upon us.

God has provided ministry gifts, or positions of ministry, for the strength, health, maturity, and leadership of the Church. Throughout this study we will continue to see how beautifully God has provided for the needs of His people by the anointing and empowerment of His Spirit.

THE POWER GIFTS

Faith

Faith comes first in this triad of the *power gifts*. This spiritual gift of faith is to be distinguished from faith without which it is impossible to please God.

✎ **1. Read Romans 1:17; Ephesians 2:8; and Hebrews 11:6. How is the "faith" referred to in these verses unique from the "gift of faith" in 1 Corinthians 12:9?**

_____

_____

_____

A specific kind of faith is necessary for the salvation of the soul. "The just shall live by faith" is the fundamental principle of the Christian life, but this is not, as we shall see, the spiritual *gift* of faith. The wording of 1 Corinthians 12:9 indicates that not all will receive this special gift from the Holy Spirit. Weymouth translates: "To a third man, by means of the same Spirit, special faith."

Donald Gee, a pioneer in the Pentecostal movement, put it this way: "The spiritual gift of faith is a special quality of faith, sometimes called by our older theologians the *faith of miracles*. It would seem to come upon certain of God's servants in times of special crisis or opportunity in such mighty power that they are lifted right out of the realm of even natural and ordinary faith in God—and have a divine certainty put within their souls that triumphs over everything."

✎ **2. Read the following passages, and then summarize the reasons special faith was needed in each circumstance and the actions required on the part of those given this *power gift* of faith.**

Genesis 6:1 to 7:5 _____

_____

1 Kings 18:1-26 _____

_____

2 Kings 3:16-20 _____

_____

Daniel 3:1-30_____

_____

Daniel 6:1-28_____

_____

This special *gift of faith* has been in evidence throughout the ages. The examples just given are but a few Old Testament incidents which demonstrate this fact.

✎ 3. Read Matthew 17:20 and Mark 11:22. Describe the faith Jesus encouraged His disciples to exhibit.

_____

_____

_____

When the *gift of faith* is in operation, it moves the hand of God on our behalf. It is as if the currency of heaven is faith. If we ask according to God's will and purpose combined with our faithfulness, we can expect God to be true to His promises and exhibit His faithfulness to us.

Miracles

The phrase generally translated in 1 Corinthians 12:10 as "the working of miracles" (KJV) or "miraculous powers" (NIV) literally means "energies of power" (both nouns in the plural). Dr. A. S. Way translates it: "energies of supernatural power"; Weymouth: "exercise of miraculous powers"; Goodspeed: "the working of wonders." A clear rendering would be "operations of works of power." The emphasis is upon phenomena produced by supernatural power.

✎ 4. What is the primary effect of the coming of the Holy Spirit promised in Acts 1:8?

_____

_____

_____

_____

What is a miraculous event? Webster's Dictionary states, "A miracle is an event or effect in the physical world deviating from the known laws of nature, or transcending our knowledge of these laws." The Scriptures, both Old and New Testament, are full of accounts of the miraculous working of God through His servants, as well as of the sovereign working of His power directly.

✎ 5. Read the following Scripture passages and record each miracle that took place and the reason why the event should be classified as a miracle:

Exodus 7:10,20_____

_____

_____

2 Kings 6:1-7 _____

_____

_____

Acts 9:40 _____

_____

_____

Acts 19:11,12 _____

_____

_____

Acts 20:10 _____

_____

_____

6. Describe God's power at work found in the following Scripture passages:

Acts 5:17-25 _____

_____

_____

Acts 12:3-12 _____

_____

_____

Acts 16:16-40 _____

_____

_____

When there was need for the display of His power to further His divine purposes for His servants, and His Church—God showed it. We can take courage in the fact that God is still willing to do the same for His followers today.

Healings
The spiritual *gifts of healings* are given to confirm the gospel message and to alleviate suffering for God's glory. But, like every other gift, they lie in the sovereignty of God. Note again that both words in this designation are in the plural num-

ber—*gifts (charismata) of healings*. This bestowment is not to be construed as a gift by which the possessor can heal all cases of sickness without exception. God has made resident in His Church potentialities of healing the sick which are exercised by certain Spirit-filled believers.

✎ 7. Read Mark 16:17,18 and James 5:14,15. What prayer formula is suggested for someone who is sick?

_____

_____

As noted above, the gifts are to confirm the Word of God, to prepare hearts to receive the gospel, and to bring glory to God. To hold this view of the gifts will make full room for the sovereignty of God. It will prevent disappointment and disillusionment by those who do not receive physical healing. It will keep those who are used to pray for the sick and who do see many healed humble. Most important, this understanding will keep us in a proper spiritual balance.

ADDITIONAL MINISTRY GIFTS

All too often in Pentecostal circles, the spiritual gifts are limited to the list found in 1 Corinthians 12. Perhaps many are unaware that equally important lists of gifts exist elsewhere in the New Testament. We will turn our attention to some of those at this time.

✎ 8. Compare the following Scripture passages and make a list of similarities and differences concerning spiritual gifts you discover in each set of Scripture passages.

1 Corinthians 12:8-10 and Romans 12:6-8 _____

_____

_____

Romans 12:6-8 and 1 Corinthians 12:28 _____

_____

_____

The similarities which you just discovered indicate the latter group are in the same category of importance as the former.

Paul's *body* symbolism helps us to see that although members of the Body will have different functions and degrees of prominence, each must exercise his spiritual gifts recognizing the mutual dependence of each member of the Body. All gifts should be exercised in faith, within each believer's limits, with an unselfish attitude to replace any member's exercise of unwarranted authority.

Ministry Or Service

The word *ministry*, from the Greek *diakonia*, is a broad term appearing regularly in the New Testament in connection with service in the Church. Its precise meaning is unclear in Romans 12:7, but it is used of service in general, including all forms of Christian service tending to the good of the Christian body.

9. Read the following Scripture passages and record how you could render a similar type of service today.

Acts 6:1-3 _____

_____

Acts 20:24 _____

_____

2 Corinthians 5:18-20 _____

_____

Ephesians 4:11-13 _____

_____

James: 1:26,27 _____

_____

_____

The Lord has blessed certain individuals who are ready and willing to fit in anywhere in joyous service to the body of Christ. We each need to be consecrated to whatever service the Lord has for us, regardless if it is public or hidden.

Teaching

The ministry of the teacher, which Christ has provided His Church, is a very important one. On one hand it is filled with limitless possibilities of blessing, guidance, and instruction; on the other hand it has a potential for danger. Someone said it is teachers who have been responsible for some of the schisms in the Church. Not those who occupied a place in the classroom, but those in a leadership role who were responsible to lay foundational interpretations of Scripture, etc.

10. Read James 3:1. What do these words communicate to those who wish to teach concerning the importance of the function and the seriousness with which one should undertake the task?

_____

_____

_____

May the Lord help, guide, and keep humble the teacher whose office is often combined with that of pastor. This office has not always been appreciated, for the appeal is to the intellect in making truth clearly understood. But this ministry is extremely vital. The truth has to be first understood before it can impact the soul and be accepted by the will.

New converts need to be grounded in the principles of the faith and guided in their walk. To fulfill this ministry there must be a *charisma*–a gracious enabling of God!

Exhortation

"Exhortation is such a distinctive phase of the gift of prophecy (see 1 Corinthians 14:3) that it is dignified by being called a gift (*charisma*) itself. Here is the emotional appeal characteristic of the 'gifts' of utterance, not just an emotional outburst by way of relief for pent-up feelings. It is a controlled stream of earnest, vibrant Holy Spirit words directed to sinner or saint with a plea to turn from wrong to right, from error to truth, to obedience and faith. God loves and God pleads (by means of exhortation exercised) through the 'gift' of prophecy."—Ralph Riggs, in *The Spirit Himself.*

11. What surprising "gift" is highlighted in 2 Corinthians 8:1-7?

_____

_____

Christian Benevolence

In the apostle Paul's second letter to the Corinthians, the classic chapters on Christian benevolence distinctly refer to this practical manifestation of love and unselfishness as a grace (*charis*).

12. Read 2 Corinthians 8:1 through 9:15. Summarize the principles of giving outlined in these chapters as well as the benefits available to those who participate.

_____

_____

_____

_____

When someone opens his heart completely in personal consecration, including the sharing of his finances, he is blessed of God in this ministry and occupies an important place in the divine economy. Here is a gift every one of God's children can receive and express with simplicity and generosity. In so doing it brings glory to God and helps carry out His program.

Administration

God has designed His Church to have individuals in leadership who are responsible for guiding and directing the activities of the church locally and around the world.

✎ 13. From Romans 12:8 and 1 Thessalonians 5:12, what words are used to describe the *gift of administration?*

_____

_____

The Giver of the ministry-gifts is our exalted Lord, Jesus Christ, who came from the Heavenly Father and completed the plan of redemption. This exalted Christ granted the Church leaders with specific functions.

✎ 14. According to Ephesians 4:11-13, what ministry (leadership) roles did God give the Church and for what functions?

_____

_____

Such people have great responsibility and are exhorted to govern diligently, and earnestly, realizing the responsibility God granted them and the urgency of the eternal issues.

Our Lord never intended that a one-man ministry reign over His Church. This prevalent and distorted idea has disappointed some people expecting a pastor, for example, to be a combination of all of these ministries. Furthermore, this concept has put a heavy strain upon the pastor himself. It is a rare person who can fulfill the requirements of evangelist, pastor, teacher, and prophet. Our Lord's intention is clear that there should be a distribution of these ministries not only in the Church-at-large, but in the local assembly. Let's look at each of these ministry functions.

Apostles

The root meaning of the Greek word *apostolos* is "a messenger, a sent one." Its Latin counterpart means "missionary." Christ himself was an Apostle, a Missionary, a Sent One, commissioned of the Father to carry out His redemptive purpose (Hebrews 3:1).

✎ 15. What special place and significance do the 12 apostles and Paul have in God's overall plan according to 1 Corinthians 3:10; Ephesians 2:20; and Revelation 21:14?

_____

_____

_____

In a unique sense Christ chose, trained, and sent forth a group of men whose work was to be foundational to the Church. He also called, separated, and commissioned Paul to be an apostle to the Gentiles. These men were foundation stones in the Church structure and always will occupy that unique place.

It is clear there were other men called apostles in the sense of being pioneers, founders of churches, etc. (Acts 14:14; 1 Corinthians 15:7-9). Only the 12 apostles however, have the above unique distinction. The Lord may raise up men in these last days with apostolic dignity and power. They will be recognized not by the assumption of a title, but by the manifestation of spiritual power.

Prophets

The *prophets* are those who have a ministry similar to that of Old Testament prophets. The prophet was one who spoke from the impulse of a sudden inspiration, from the light of a sudden revelation at the moment.

The *prophets* are distinguished from teachers in the Early Church. The teacher's ministry is more logical, appealing to the reasoning faculties of the hearers; the prophet's appeal is to the conscience more generally through the emotions. *Prophets* are distinguished from evangelists in that while the latter may be powerful emotional preachers, they do not necessarily minister from an immediate revelation at the moment.

Evangelists

The word *evangelist* occurs but three times in the New Testament.

16. What do Acts 21:8; Ephesians 4:11; and 2 Timothy 4:5 have to say about the *evangelist*?

_____

_____

_____

The term *evangelist* means "one who brings good tidings." Philip exemplified the scriptural norm of the true evangelist. His ministry was supernaturally advertised, he was accredited by God, and his message was authenticated by the signs which accompanied his preaching (Acts 8:6-8). The *evangelist* is also a personal worker, for the Lord led Philip to the Ethiopian eunuch.

Pastors

The word *pastor* occurs in the New Testament only in Ephesians 4:11, but the concept of the word is found everywhere. The Greek word means "shepherd." God is seen in many Old Testament verses as the Shepherd feeding, guiding, protecting His flock (Psalm 23), and indicting the hirelings who failed to do this. Christ is the Great Shepherd of His people.

17. Look up John 10:11; Hebrews 13:20; and 1 Peter 2:25; 5:4. What do these verses say about Jesus' shepherding role?

_____

_____

_____

Just as sheep need oversight, care, and protection, so do believers gathered in local churches need leaders with hearts of true shepherds to exercise loving oversight over them.

✎ 18. List some of the responsibilities of pastors mentioned in Matthew 24:45; Acts 20:28; 1 Corinthians 14:40; Titus 1:9,11; Hebrews 13:17; James 5:14; 1 Peter 5:2; and 2 Peter 2:1.

_____

_____

_____

_____

Donald Gee makes this observation concerning the pastoral role: "There is always the need of wise and competent oversight of the meetings of the assembly, so that all things are done 'decently and in order'; so that the doctrine is kept sound and convincing; and so that the flock be preserved from wolves in the shape of false teachers. There will also be the need of personal ministration to the members in times of special individual need and of a loving care over all the souls for which these spiritual rulers in the Master's household will have to give an account. Above all else, will be the positive work of feeding the flock, because a flock well fed is least likely to become unhealthy spiritually or to give any trouble."

Teachers
The ministry-gift of teaching held an important and specific place in the New Testament Church, proven by its mention in all three ministries' lists given respectively in Romans 12; 1 Corinthians 12; and Ephesians 4. In the Greek text, Paul groups "pastors and teachers" together, implying these two offices were often united in one person. Blessed indeed is the assembly whose pastor has a shepherd's heart and a teaching gift.

A teacher, if really given by Christ and anointed by the Holy Spirit, can be of inestimable blessing and profit to the Church.

✎ 19. Compare John 7:38 with 1 Corinthians 3:6. How does the imagery of these two verses help define the purpose and value of the teacher?

_____

_____

SUMMARY

Each of the gifts of the Spirit work together to provide a well-rounded and firmly grounded body of believers. Each gift plays an important role in communicating God's love to the world. Followers of Jesus, who have been baptized in the Holy Spirit, should seek those spiritual gifts God has for them.

LET'S REVIEW

1. Give examples of how the *gift of faith* is beyond the simple faith for salvation.

_____

_____

_____

2. Define *working of miracles* and give examples.

_____

_____

_____

3. Discuss the limitations and purpose of the *gifts of healings.*

_____

_____

_____

4. Detail the *gift of prophecy* as explained in Romans 12:4-8.

_____

_____

_____

5. Discuss ways you have been used by God as a result of a spiritual gift He has given to you.

_____

_____

_____

_____

_____

ADMINISTERING THE SPIRITUAL GIFTS

I t is obvious from their very nature that the spiritual gifts God has given His Church are supernatural and miraculous. Consequently, their exercise in the gatherings of God's people should be a thrilling experience. But we must remember the gifts are exercised through human channels, which at best are "earthen vessels," frail and imperfect (2 Corinthians 4:7). We must also recognize they are not manifested mechanically through unfeeling instruments but through intelligent beings. The Holy Spirit seeks the cooperation of the Spirit-filled believer in administering these gifts in order that the Church may be edified, our Lord Jesus Christ glorified, and the kingdom of God extended.

THE PROPER MOTIVE

Motivation is something within an individual which incites him to an action, such as any idea, need, emotion, or natural state. If a motive is wrong, the results of that motive will sometimes be wrong. We must carefully examine and evaluate our motives when exercising them.

There are no specific instructions in Scripture for the administration of the gifts of power and of revelation. Paul, however, felt it was imperative to write instructions concerning the use and abuse of the speech gifts. First Corinthians 14 (the primary chapter which deals with the administration of spiritual gifts) was written by Paul to Corinth because the gifts of tongues and of prophecy were being abused.

Preceding chapter 14 is the directly connected classic 13th chapter of 1 Corinthians. Chapter 13 is not an isolated *hymn to love*, but an integral part of the entire theme of the spiritual gifts. Note the last verse of chapter 12 naturally leads into chapter 13. Then note how the first verse of chapter 14 leads naturally out of chapter 13.

The "most excellent way" of 1 Corinthians 13 is a path which leads to the goal of edification, profit, peace, and order. Without this love, the whole complement of spiritual gifts can accomplish nothing of real spiritual worth.

✎ **1. Read 1 Corinthians 14:5,12,19,26. According to these verses, what is the primary purpose of love-motivated spiritual gifts?**

_____

_____

_____

Edification is like a building gradually rising from a strong foundation until the whole building is completed. Spiritual gifts are to be exercised so the whole Church may be built up, with each member pressing toward spiritual perfection, which is the heartbeat of the Master Architect. Our pattern is the Lord Jesus Christ, into whose likeness we are to grow.

✎ **2. In 1 Corinthians 12:7, who does Paul say is to be the beneficiary of spiritual gifts?**

_____

_____

Spiritual gifts are not designed exclusively for the benefit, or even the gratification, of those through whom the Spirit exercises them. They are bestowed for the good of the whole Church. "Just as the power of vision is not for the benefit of the eye, but for the man himself. When, therefore, the gifts of God, natural or supernatural, are perverted as means of self-exaltation or aggrandizement, it is a sin against their Giver, as well as against those for whose benefit they were intended."—Charles Hodge.

THE PROPER USE

Many have relegated spiritual gifts to the period of the Early Church. They feel the operation of the gifts has already ceased. Those who believe this base their theology on a misunderstanding of 1 Corinthians 13:8-13.

✎ 3. Read 1 Corinthians 13:8-13. Some teach that the term "the perfect" refers to the completed text of the Bible, thus when the Bible was complete, spiritual gifts were no longer needed. In the context of the entire paragraph (especially verse 12), what was Paul actually referring to as "the perfect" and why will spiritual gifts no longer be needed in that context?

_____

_____

_____

One of the favorite targets of those who would relegate the spiritual gifts to the Early Church is the practice of speaking in tongues. These individuals are unaware of what they miss from not participating in this experience. What a spiritually satisfying experience it is to be able to express our deepest feelings toward God even beyond our understanding. We should worship, praise, and petition God in language that can be understood. But some things require a more adequate channel for expression.

✎ 4. Read Romans 8:26. How does the Holy Spirit help the Spirit-filled believer who is struggling to express himself to God?

_____

_____

Speaking in tongues is God's chosen method of communicating between the very soul of man and himself when situations occur which are beyond a person's human comprehension.

Speaking in tongues is not limited to personal interaction with God. Speaking in tongues also plays a vital role in the life of the gathered body of Christ. Paul points out, however, that the use of the gift of speaking in tongues in a corporate setting must be with wisdom and in love.

✎ 5. Read 1 Corinthians 14:22. According to Paul, how might speaking in tongues be viewed by the unbeliever?

_____

_____

_____

What does Paul mean by his assertion in 1 Corinthians 14:22? Perhaps Paul envisioned occasions prompted by the Holy Spirit–such as the Day of Pentecost–when a known language might be spoken. It would be intelligible to the unbeliever because it was his native tongue. Multiplied instances of such remarkable manifestations have occurred in the modern Pentecostal movement and many people have been converted as a result.

Paul next turns his attention to the proper use of the spiritual gift of prophecy. Paul gives it first place among the speech gifts. Compared to the ministry of the teacher, who engages the understanding and the intellect, prophecy appeals to the emotions and excites what teaching enlightens. These two offices were beautifully combined in the Early Church at Antioch (see Acts 13:1).

✎ 6. According to 1 Corinthians 14:3,24, what positive results should occur when a prophetic message is given in a spirit of love?

_____

_____

Prophecy can lift the assembly into heights of glory and enthusiasm, warm its heart with tenderness, or cause trembling with the awe of God's presence. Prophecy is to be diligently sought and earnestly desired.

THE PROPER EXERCISE

The scene in the Corinthian assembly was one of confusion. There were various spiritual exercises occurring at the same time, with no consideration for anyone else.

✎ 7. According to 1 Corinthians 14:40, what is the key to the proper exercise of the spiritual gifts in a worship service?

_____

There should be liberty for the exercise of spiritual gifts, but this liberty does not include abuse of others for personal gratification. The whole universe evidences divine order. The sun rises and sets; the phases of the moon follow each other in regular sequence; the seasons come and go. The individual planets and stars, even whole galaxies, move in one grand procession in their orbits.

✎ 8. How does the illustration given in 1 Corinthians 12:12-28 help one's understanding of God and the proper exercise of spiritual gifts?

_____

_____

_____

If Christians fail to recognize their vital relationship to one another as members of one Body, and to Christ, the Head, the spiritual gifts will lose their effectiveness. It is necessary for all members of the Body, whether or not they are distinctive, to function in order that the whole Body may grow and become healthy.

By not maintaining the recommended control over their spirits, those who prophesied at Corinth were not true prophets. By giving in to their impulse to speak in an unbridled way, there arose a state of confusion and disorder that could not possibly come from God. That peace, which is essentially God's work, would be broken up. God is not a God of confusion. He is the "God of peace" and order (Romans 15:33).

As we have seen, because of the problems which occurred in the Corinthian church, Paul outlined rules to regulate the use of the speech gifts. These rules are as important today as they were in the first century. Let's first look at the rules governing speaking in tongues.

Speaking in tongues was a cause of spiritual pride in the Corinthian church. It seems the more often one spoke in tongues during the assembly, the more spiritual the speaker felt. Church services at Corinth began to resemble the competition in the athletic contests commonly associated with the nearby city of Athens.

Spiritual gifts, though empowered by the Holy Spirit, operate through the human spirit. They are effective, profitable, and bring blessing when exercised through yielded, cooperative, clean, love-filled vessels.

9. Read 1 Corinthians 14:22-28. How does Paul resolve the problem of wholesale speaking in tongues in the church service?

_____

Any human tendency to explain this as two or three persons but unlimited number of expressions renders these wonderful exercises common and pointless.

10. According to 1 Corinthians 14:6-21, why does Paul demand an interpretation if a tongue is spoken?

_____

_____

11. In spite of the potential problems with speaking in tongues in a worship setting, what does Paul declare regarding speaking in tongues in 1 Corinthians 14:39,40?

_____

Now let's turn our attention to Paul's counsel concerning the spiritual gift of prophecy.

One of the values, as well as the dangers, of prophecy is the authority by which it is given. When an individual properly gives a prophetic word, he or she is speaking on behalf of God. Unfortunately, not all prophets are true prophets. Prophetic messages must be weighed carefully because they are exercised through imperfect human agents. The Scriptures clearly state that prophetic utterances may emanate from the human spirit (see Jeremiah 23:16; Ezekiel 13:2,3).

✎ 12. According to 1 Corinthians 14:29, what spiritual safeguard has God put in place to ensure the accuracy of a prophetic utterance?

_____

_____

✎ 13. How do 1 Corinthians 12:3,10 and 1 John 4:1-6 help us in properly evaluating the gift of prophecy?

_____

_____

✎ 14. What additional insights can be gained from a reading of 1 Corinthians 14:12 regarding the evaluation of prophetic messages?

_____

_____

_____

Consider the truth that spiritual gifts are not infallible. Human vessels through which they operate are faulty and frail, yet these gifts need to be regulated and exercised in love and humility.

It is interesting to note that Paul used the word "excel" in his instructions concerning spiritual gifts (1 Corinthians 14:12). The word *excel* implies we may surpass present achievement. This goal may be realized in regard to spiritual gifts by humbly and prayerfully seeking the Lord that we may become pure, yielded, and wiser vessels for the Holy Spirit.

SUMMARY

Every Spirit-filled believer should be keenly aware and intensely desirous of glorifying his Master. God has blessed His Church with certain gifts and enablements for her own spiritual benefit and growth. These gifts and enablements will arm her for battle against satanic powers and provide for the advancement of Christ's kingdom. Because of the reality of this truth, every believer should seek the Lord for spiritual gifts as the Holy Spirit provides.

Spirit-filled believers should also recognize that God wishes His followers to exercise the gifts given to them in freedom and liberty. This can only be accomplished, however, when abuses are controlled by divine regulations. Consequently, the regulations discussed in this study should be seen as keys to freedom rather than handcuffs which hinder spiritual expression. The Holy Spirit is both gentle and strict. He demands that all things associated with Him "be done in a fitting and orderly way" (1 Corinthians 14:40, NIV).

LET'S REVIEW

1. How does the message of 1 Corinthians 13 influence Paul's regulations concerning the spiritual gifts recorded in 1 Corinthians 14?

_____

_____

_____

2. What general rules should govern speaking in tongues in a general assembly according to Paul?

_____

_____

_____

3. What rules should govern prophetic utterances according to Paul?

_____

_____

_____

4. What spiritual result should occur from a prophetic utterance if given according to God's love?

_____

_____

_____

5. What are some biblical ways to evaluate if a spiritual gift is truly from God?

_____

_____

_____

_____

SPIRITUAL CAUTIONS

The Holy Spirit is Deity, the Third Person of the Trinity, and the only One through whom conviction of sin can come. It is disastrous to blaspheme, resist, or grieve Him, or to quench His operations. Two of these four cautions concern the sinner. The other two admonitions concern those who are children of God. It is extremely important that everyone, Christian or not, understand what the Bible teaches concerning treatment of God's Spirit. These truths should be clearly understood by all so the proper attitude and respect can be shown. Let's look at each in turn.

DON'T RESIST THE HOLY SPIRIT

The God of the universe maintains communication with a fallen world by means of His Holy Spirit. To resist the Holy Spirit is a severe sin. It is resisting the very means by which God provides recovery for human souls and brings them into relationship with Jesus Christ.

✎ 1. Read John 16:8-11. Record the reason given in this passage for the Holy Spirit's coming to the earth.

_____

_____

The Spirit not only convicts and reproves, but lovingly, earnestly, and tenderly brings the sinner to repentance. The Spirit presents the consequences of unbelief and resistance to Christ and attempts to turn the sinner away from sin and over to Christ.

✎ 2. Compare the following accounts and record the response of those confronted with their sin.

Luke 19:1-9 _____

Acts 6:8 to 7:54 _____

In Acts 6:8 through 7:54 members of the Sanhedrin provide an example of individuals who resisted the loving reproof of the Holy Spirit. They earlier rejected the person of Jesus and then rejected the message of the Cross.

✎ 3. How does Stephen's description of the Sanhedrin found in Acts 7:51 characterize individuals who refuse to heed the conviction of the Holy Spirit?

_____

_____

Israel resisted her prophets. Jeremiah was thrust into prison and his feet placed in the stocks. He was cast into a pit and would have perished had not Ebedmelech, the Ethiopian, rescued him. Isaiah, according to tradition, was sawed apart by order of the wicked King Manasseh. Israel hated the prophets and their message, because they disturbed the conscience of the nation and temporarily aroused them from their chosen spiritual stupor.

The crowning sin of Israel was rejecting their Messiah. He represented, in His teachings, in His acts of mercy, sympathy, and love, everything that was noble, pure, and good. In the same way, many today resist the Messiah and His messenger.

One of the primary ways of resisting the Messiah today is through inattention and neglect. To be attentive is to closely observe what is being said or done. It is possible to hear and yet not to hear and not have what is said really register upon the consciousness. Until one truly hears, no emotional response or act of the will follows.

Occasionally, inattention is preceded by an act of the will which determines not to give notice and comes from a stubborn spirit. This rebellious spirit, which refused God's message through the prophets, characterized Israel and brought many calamities upon their heads as the Scripture records.

✎ 4. How does 1 Samuel 15:23 describe the sin of rebellion? To broaden your understanding, look at the rendering of this verse in a variety of translations.

_____

_____

DON'T BLASPHEME THE HOLY SPIRIT

All blasphemy against the Holy Spirit is sin; but not all sin against the Holy Spirit is blasphemy. This fact narrows blasphemy to a particular sin. What is it? To speak abusive words against God willfully, knowingly, and malignantly is blasphemy.

✎ 5. Read Matthew 12:31,32; Mark 3:28,29; and Luke 12:10. What is the consequence of blaspheming the Holy Spirit?

_____

_____

Matthew 12:22-37 tells how Christ cast a demon from a man who was blind and dumb, and then the man both saw and spoke. Most people were amazed at this wonderful miracle and were inclined to accept Christ as the Son of David, the Messiah. But the Pharisees attributed Christ's work to His having a connection with Beelzebub, a heathen deity, supposedly the prince of the demons. The parallel passage in Mark 3 indicates they attributed Christ's miraculous powers to an alliance with Satan.

What is the difference, then, between speaking against the Son of Man and speaking against the Holy Spirit? Speaking against the Son of Man is a reproach on the Savior's person, challenging the significance of His birth, etc. But by speaking against the Holy Spirit, the speaker is blaspheming the divine power whereby Christ performed His miracles. This is not a sin which one can commit by accident and without knowing it. It is the result of a long series of rebellious acts.

Why is this sin so terrible and not the sin against the Father or the Son? Is the Holy Spirit more sacred than they? No, for all are equal in glory. But when the gospel is maligned, the Holy Spirit is especially opposed. It is a defiance of His special authority and of the only One who can make a sinner conscious of his need. It is the divine Spirit who takes the things of Christ and presents them to the soul.

Why is such a sin unpardonable? Because of the nature of a heart resolutely opposed to the Spirit and the truth. Pardon is forgiveness. God does not forgive unless we sincerely ask for it. If we turn our backs and the Spirit is scorned, pardon is impossible. As sorrow for sin is unknown to those guilty of blasphemy against the Holy Spirit, their salvation is impossible.

DON'T GRIEVE THE HOLY SPIRIT

We may anger a stranger, but we grieve only a friend or loved one. It is clear proof of the personality of the Holy Spirit that He can be grieved. He must take a very tender and affectionate interest in us, since He is grieved by our shortcomings and our sins.

6. What was the spiritual condition of those to whom Paul wrote concerning grieving the Holy Spirit in Ephesians 4:30? What warning does this provide for the Christian?

_____

_____

To what may the loving grief of the Holy Spirit be traced? To His holy character and perfect attributes. It is the nature of a holy being to be grieved with unholiness. This is understandable even in ourselves as Christians. We have been made partakers of the divine nature. As that nature matures, we become more and more repulsed by any conduct that violates the standards of the divine nature and of God's holy law.

It is mainly for our sakes that the Spirit is grieved. He desires us to be sensitive to things which He, as a holy Being approves, and also to those things He disapproves. He is also grieved for the Church's sake, for she is God's witness to Christ in an ungodly world. Every lapse into sin and inconsistency on the part of any individual believer weakens the corporate testimony of the Church.

7. Read the two verses on either side of the warning about grieving the Spirit (Ephesians 4:29,31). Make a list of specific sins that are offensive to the Holy Spirit. Remember that this list is not exhaustive but representative of the type of activity and attitudes that grieve the Holy Spirit.

_____

_____

_____

Clearly the Holy Spirit is grieved by unholy desires and states of mind which permit unholy words and violent conduct to occur. Christians are to be separated from the world, its pleasures, its spirit, and its program.

8. According to John 15:19; 2 Corinthians 6:14-17; and 1 John 2:15, what should the Christian's relationship be with the world?

_____

_____

An unholy love excites a holy jealousy on the part of the Holy Spirit, who is concerned that our Lord shall have all the love of the Christian.

What would grieve a parent more than to have his child doubt his truthfulness? The Holy Spirit is grieved by our occasional lack of counting God true to His Word. Unbelief cuts us off completely from His fellowship.

Nothing grieves a friend more than ingratitude for favors bestowed or gifts given. Lack of thankfulness to God for all His lovingkindness and tender mercy must grieve the Holy Spirit.

Lack of prayer is one of the clearest evidences on the part of a Christian of self-sufficiency. The prayerless Christian seems to say to the Lord, "I can get along quite well without You." In reality, we should recognize that we are dependent upon God for the very breath which sustains us.

The Christian who is guilty of grieving the Holy Spirit must expect at least a partial loss of the sense of His presence. This is serious, for perhaps the choicest blessing we can have in this life is the presence of the Lord in sacred fellowship. We should cherish this privilege above all else.

Coincidental with the absence of the presence of the Lord is losing real Christian joy, power, assurance, and usefulness for God.

✎ **9. Read the set of parables found in Luke 15:1-31. Summarize the message of hope found in the parables for those who have grieved the Holy Spirit.**

_____

_____

When the Holy Spirit comes to abide in the believer at salvation, He stamps the soul with a seal identifying a special relationship between that person and God (Ephesians 1:13; 4:30; 2 Corinthians 1:21,22).

Sealing distinguishes something as a personal possession. The affixing of a seal to a book, a mailbag, lumber, or a document, marks it as somebody's private possession. When the Holy Spirit is given to us we are set apart as God's own. Surely we do not want to do anything that will break this seal and evidence of divine ownership!

This present sealing is a foretaste of that final sealing of the redeemed as John views them in Revelation 22:4. How we should cherish the present sealing that it might find its fulfillment in that future glorious and eternal one!

Sealing is also suggestive of value or treasure. We do not seal, for example, an unimportant letter, but something valuable. The very fact the Father sends the Holy Spirit, the Third Person of the Godhead himself, to seal the soul with His presence, testifies we are of infinite value to Him.

DON'T QUENCH THE HOLY SPIRIT

Another warning to the Christian is to avoid quenching the Holy Spirit (1 Thessalonians 5:19). The original language of this passage states, "Do not put out the Spirit's fire" with a continuous sense of "stop quenching the Spirit or not to have the habit of doing it." It seems evident then, the Thessalonians were doing this very thing. The context, especially verse 20, indicates that this "quenching" was repressing the manifestation of the gifts of the Spirit.

✎ 10. Read 1 Thessalonians 5:20. What did the Thessalonians appear to be doing which would fall into the category of quenching the Holy Spirit?

_____

_____

This was the opposite of the conditions in Corinth where wild excess was rampant. In Thessalonica there was a spirit of cold indifference. It is easy for a gathering of God's people to put out the fire of spiritual fervor and power. In doing so they suffer a tragic loss. Note, however, Paul does not condone unconditional acceptance of every spiritual thing that is labeled as being from the Holy Spirit.

✎ 11. Read 1 Thessalonians 5:21. What balance is called for in this verse?

_____

_____

As Pentecostal believers, we must be sensitive to the moving and direction of the Holy Spirit. Many individuals avoid spiritual expressions because they fear excesses that they have seen or heard about in the past. We can take comfort in the fact that the Holy Spirit is a gentleman who does everything in an orderly fashion (1 Corinthians 14:20). If we yield to His leading and respond as He prompts, we can be assured that our spiritual expressions will be appropriate.

Sitting in judgment on the outward expressions of others can be equally as damaging.

✎ 12. Read 2 Samuel 6:16-23. What happened to Michal as a result of her judgmental attitude? What warning does this provide for us today?

_____

_____

God has put spiritual leaders in place to administer excesses within the Church. Our concern should not be concentrated on the actions of others nor should we attempt to make the spiritual expression of others conform to our expectations. Rather, our responsibility is to be personally responsive to the Holy Spirit's activity in our own lives.

SUMMARY

Since the Holy Spirit is not a mere influence, but a divine Person–one with the Father and the Son in the Godhead–He must be so regarded. He is the divine Administrator in this present day when God is gathering His people through the ministry of that same Spirit. His dignity and power must be recognized. To reject Him, to resist Him, to grieve, or to quench Him, is a fatal step indeed.

LET'S REVIEW

1. What does it mean to resist the Holy Spirit? Cite a biblical example.

_____

_____

_____

2. Describe the sin of blasphemy against the Holy Spirit. What makes blasphemy so awful?

_____

_____

_____

3. What does it mean to grieve the Holy Spirit? Give several examples whereby He may be grieved.

_____

_____

_____

4. What does it mean to quench the Holy Spirit and in what way may this be done?

_____

_____

_____

5. What are some practical steps we can take to ensure we do not grieve or quench the Holy Spirit?

_____

_____

_____

_____